Louis J. Holmes

A DICTIONARY OF ECONOMIC

TERMS

978 0710061003

D1744320

A
DICTIONARY
OF
ECONOMIC
TERMS

by

P A S TAYLOR
BSC(ECON), FCCS, FSS

*Senior Lecturer in Business Studies
Garnett College*

LONDON
ROUTLEDGE & KEGAN PAUL

A DICTIONARY OF ECONOMIC TERMS

First published in 1905
by George Routledge and Sons

Reprinted seven times

Second edition (revised) 1936

Reprinted 1940

Third edition (revised) 1951

Published by Routledge and Kegan Paul Ltd.,
Broadway House, 68-74 Carter Lane,
London E.C.4, England

Reprinted seven times

Fourth edition (revised and rewritten) 1968

Reprinted 1969
by Routledge and Kegan Paul Ltd.

SBN 7100 2986 1 (c)
SBN 7100 6100 5 (p)

Printed in Great Britain
by W & J Mackay & Co Ltd, Chatham

PREFACE

Basically, this book is an abbreviated version of my *A New Dictionary of Economics* with the addition of a number of statistical terms. It is hoped that the result will be of use to the general reader and students of commerce, economics and statistics.

Cross references are indicated by capital letters.

Garnett College   P A S T
SW15

abnormal profit. See NORMAL PROFIT.

accelerator. Used in KEYNESIAN ECONOMICS to show how changes in consumer expenditure may bring about changes in new CAPITAL FORMATION. If consumer expenditure increases, the extra demand for a commodity may cause production facilities to be increased, ie new *capital formation*. Conversely, a fall in demand may result in the failure of producers to replace equipment that is worn-out (see DISINVESTMENT).

acceptance. Generally, this means the agreement of a party to a contract or other arrangement submitted to him for consideration. The term is usually used to refer to the acceptance of a bill of exchange (see COMMERCIAL BILL).

acceptance house. A firm, also called a MERCHANT BANK, which carries on the business of 'accepting' bills of exchange (see COMMERCIAL BILL) for a consideration.
Many acceptance houses today act as ISSUING HOUSES; some operate in the London Gold Market; some in the LONDON FOREIGN EXCHANGE MARKET; and they all do some ordinary banking business and act as investment advisers.

account. In book-keeping an account is a ledger record of DEBITS and CREDITS. On the STOCK EXCHANGE the term refers to the period of time in which dealings are done on a credit basis.

accrued interest. INTEREST on securities, etc, which has accumulated but which has not been paid or collected.

accumulative dividend. A dividend not paid when due to SHAREHOLDERS by a company, which has thus become a liability of the company and must be paid at some future time. See SECURITIES.

ad valorem duty and taxation. The imposition of a duty on commodities in proportion to their value.

adverse balance. See UNFAVOURABLE TRADE BALANCE.

alternate demand. The DEMAND for several ECONOMIC GOODS, which to some extent satisfy the same desire, and which can be partially substituted for one another. Thus a considerable rise in the price of beef would tend to diminish that for mutton, since both satisfy the demand for meat.

amalgamation. The process whereby two or more existing firms are merged together. See INTEGRATION.

anti-dumping duty. A tariff imposed to discourage DUMPING. See GENERAL AGREEMENT ON TARIFFS AND TRADE, etc.

application money. When a NEW ISSUE of shares is made, the issuer (see ISSUING HOUSE) asks for an amount of money that must accompany the application for an allotment of shares.

applied economics. The application of ECONOMIC THEORY to the solution of economic problems, ie to the practical problems of industry, commerce and finance.

appreciation. An increase, often permanent, in the value of a commodity.

appropriation. This is the act of setting money aside before formally authorising the spending of it.

arbitrage. The buying of something in one market to sell in another to take advantage of differences in prices.

arbitration. An arrangement whereby two parties in dispute refer it to one or more impartial persons for settlement, with formal agreement to accept the decision given. It is frequently used in the settlement of labour disputes and, to a certain extent, when there is disagreement internationally.
See COLLECTIVE BARGAINING, CONCILIATION, INDUSTRIAL COURT, JOINT INDUSTRIAL COUNCIL, etc.

arithmetic mean. The familiar average obtained by dividing the total of all values by the number of values. A *weighted* arithmetic mean takes account of the fact that in some collections of numbers some of them are more important than others. See CENTRAL TENDENCY.

array. An arrangement of data made in such a way that the first item is the lowest and the last the highest. An array may be used to locate the MEDIAN and QUARTILES.

articles of association. The rules for the management and regulation of the internal arrangements of a JOINT-STOCK company.

assembly line. A technique of production that usually involves the use of a conveyor belt to carry the work under construction past workers, each of whom performs a certain operation.
See DIVISION OF LABOUR.

assessment. A valuation for the purpose of TAXATION.

asset. Something of value that is owned. The following are the most important kinds of assets:
current asset—an asset that is temporary in nature and will be changed into cash within a short space of time;
earning asset—assets that earn, eg interest earning SECURITIES possessed by a firm;
fixed asset—a durable asset that can be used repeatedly, eg buildings, land and machinery;
floating asset—an asset that can be quickly converted into cash at or near its book value (sometimes called a 'quick' asset);

intangible asset—an asset of no material substance, eg GOOD-
WILL;
wasting asset—an irreplaceable asset, the life of which cannot
be prolonged; eg a mine.
See also FROZEN and LIQUID.

assurance. That part of the INSURANCE business that is in the
'life' branch.

attribute. A qualitative non-numerical description, eg blonde
or brunette; strongly disapprove, disapprove, indifferent, etc.

auction. A sale in which goods are sold to the highest bidder.
Auction sales fall into two categories: the more common type in
which bids begin at a low price, rise, and stop at the highest bid;
and the 'Dutch' type, in which the seller, or his agent, starts at a
high price and lowers it until a sale is made.

audit. The examination of the books of a firm by a competent
person, usually an accountant, in order to prove their accuracy
and correctness.

authorised capital. See CAPITAL.

authorised clerk. A clerk, working for a STOCKBROKER, who
is allowed to deal in the STOCK EXCHANGE.

authorised dealer. Under the EXCHANGE CONTROL a British
resident can only obtain, or dispose of, foreign currency through
an 'authorised dealer'. Most of the banks in Britain have been
appointed as such.

automation. This may be defined as a stage of industrial development beyond mechanisation in which processes are automatically adjusted to cope with deviations or variations.

average deviation. See MEAN DEVIATION.

average, to. In the STOCK EXCHANGE, the practice of buying
more of a SECURITY already held when the price of it is falling.
See also PYRAMID, TO.

'back-door' operations. When the DISCOUNT HOUSES seek
funds from the BANK OF ENGLAND they may obtain what they
need from the 'front door' by rediscounting COMMERCIAL or
TREASURY BILLS or by borrowing on the security of such bills.
An alternative procedure exists whereby the discount houses or
commercial banks are given 'temporary accommodation at the
back door (ie through the Bank of England's own broker in the
market) at a rate that does not disturb the level of the market
rates' (Sayers). See also BANK RATE and OPEN MARKET OPERA-
TIONS.

backwardation. Sometimes in the STOCK EXCHANGE it is in-
convenient or impossible for a dealer to complete a transaction

at the end of an ACCOUNT and he makes an arrangement called a 'backwardation' to carry it over into the next period for dealings.
See also CONTANGO.

balance of payments. This term refers to the difference between the total payments into and out of a country during a given period of time. These payments and receipts include all merchandise and bullion (see VISIBLES) and other items such as insurance charges, payments for shipping services, tourist expenditure, capital movements and interest charges (see INVISIBLES).

All the items affecting the current income and expenditure of a country make up the balance of payments, current account. The net result of the movement of capital into and out of the country (see CAPITAL MOVEMENT) is called the balance of payments, capital account. Both current and capital account must be used to compute a country's overall balance of payments.

If, on balance, a country is in credit it has a *favourable balance;* if it is a debtor, it has an *unfavourable balance.*

balance of trade. The difference between the monetary values of a country's VISIBLE imports and exports (see BALANCE OF PAYMENTS, FAVOURABLE and UNFAVOURABLE TRADE BALANCE).

balance sheet. A list of ASSETS and liabilities displayed at their monetary value at a given time.

Baltic Mercantile and Shipping Exchange. This business of the 'Baltic' can be described as the provision of facilities for the fixing of cargoes for merchant vessels. In addition to the chartering and purchase of ships, business is now conducted in the sale of grain, oil and oil seeds and the chartering of aircraft.

bank. A firm, usually a JOINT-STOCK company, formed to perform one or more of the following functions: provide a safe place for the deposit of cash or valuables; advance money; issue notes; facilitate payments by book-entries; discount COMMERCIAL BILLS; and act as an agent in a variety of other ways. See BANK MONEY.

bank bills. See COMMERCIAL BILLS.

Bank Charter Act, 1844. This is the most important Act of Parliament affecting the BANK OF ENGLAND.

Some of the main provisions of the Act are as follows.

(i) The Bank of England was to be divided into the Issue Department, to be concerned with the note issue; and the Banking Department, to be concerned with the ordinary banking business.

(ii) A FIDUCIARY ISSUE to be permitted of up to £14 million. All notes in excess of £14 million had to be secured by an equivalent value of BULLION.

(iii) The future issues of notes by existing banks was limited to the average circulation for a short period before the Act.

(iv) No further note-issuing banks could be established and existing note-issuing banks to lose the right of issue should then become bankrupt or amalgamate with a bank having a London branch.

(v) Once the right to issue notes had been relinquished, the Bank of England, by Order in Council, could increase the fiduciary issue by two-thirds of the lapsed issue.

The Act ensured that the issue of paper money was carefully regulated, and that information concerning issues and reserves would be available. Also, it had the effect of centralising the note issue in England and Wales, although the Bank of England did not gain a complete monopoly of this until 1921.

bank credit. CREDIT created by a bank by increasing the size of the account of a depositor, eg when making an advance, or when buying a SECURITY or COMMERCIAL BILL at a discount.

bankers' clearings. Cheques drawn on one bank and payable to an account in another are 'cleared' through CLEARING HOUSES. The most important one in Britain is the LONDON BANKERS' CLEARING HOUSE, whilst a number of 'local' clearings are carried on in the larger provincial cities.

Bank for International Settlements. The BIS was established in 1930 by representatives of the CENTRAL BANKS of Belgium, Britain, Germany, Italy and Japan, with some representation from the USA, partly to facilitate the transfer of reparation payments from Germany and partly to provide extra facilities for international payments operations. Since 1945, its activities have increased; for example, it has carried out the detailed management of the EUROPEAN MONETARY AGREEMENT and it has contributed to international monetary co-operation by assisting to smooth out temporary exchange fluctuations by entering into currency and gold 'swap' arrangements with central banks.

See also BASLE AGREEMENTS.

bank money. The final stage in the development of MONEY is the use of bank deposits as money. The device by which payments are made is called a CHEQUE, although it is the bank deposit that is considered as money. The importance of bank money is illustrated by the fact that of the total supply of money in Britain, three-quarters of it is in the form of bank money. See CASH and DEPOSIT.

bank note. A type of paper MONEY issued by a bank and carrying a promise to pay a specific amount to the bearer on demand. See PROMISSORY NOTE.

Bank of England. The 'Old Lady of Threadneedle Street' was founded in 1694, when in return for a loan of £1,200,000 to the government of William III at 8 per cent, a charter was granted giving the privilege of incorporation. The charter was renewed many times subsequently in return for further loans and the Bank of England remained a private institution until 1946, when it was nationalised. From its foundation, the Bank has acted as the bank of the British government, and, as such, receives the revenue of the government, and makes payments as instructed. The Bank still lends money directly to the government, by means of WAYS AND MEANS ADVANCES. Another important function of the Bank is that of the sole issuer of notes in England and Wales (see BANK CHARTER ACT). Like all CENTRAL BANKS it acts as banker to the 'commercial' banks. That is, it maintains accounts in the names of these banks, and inter-bank indebtedness can be settled merely by book entries. See CLEARING BANKS and CLEARING HOUSE. The bank also acts as the 'lender of last resort' to assist the banking system in time of crisis. In Britain, this function operates mainly through the DISCOUNT HOUSES. See also BANK RATE.

The Bank of England plays an important role by implementing the monetary policy of the government. Both before and after its nationalisation in 1946, the Bank co-operated closely with the Treasury to influence the economy. The monetary policy is carried out through the Bank's control of the banking system and the main weapons that are used are bank rate, OPEN MARKET OPERATIONS, 'BACK-DOOR' OPERATIONS and SPECIAL DEPOSITS.

The external business of the Bank has been summarised as follows:

(i) the management of the EXCHANGE EQUALISATION ACCOUNT;

(ii) administration of EXCHANGE CONTROL;

(iii) relations, both operational and diplomatic, with monetary authorities in other *sterling area* countries (see SCHEDULED TERRITORIES);

(iv) relations, partly operational and partly informational, with central banks in non-sterling countries; and

(v) participation in the work of certain international financial institutions.

bank of issue. A bank able to issue notes.

bank rate. This is the official minimum rate per cent at which the BANK OF ENGLAND will discount first-class COMMERCIAL BILLS. Traditionally, bank rate is the main instrument used by central banks to control the price of CREDIT and thus the volume of credit and the monetary situation in general.

The bank rate influences many other rates of interest so that when it is raised, borrowing is made more expensive, the demand for loans falls, and business activity tends to be reduced. A lower bank rate means that borrowing is cheaper. and that an expansion of credit is encouraged, but it does not follow that there will necessarily be an increase in borrowing, because of business pessimism.

Bank rate can be an unreliable instrument of control. The effects of rises are usually more predictable, but many people agree that a rise in the bank rate is symbolical and evidence that the authorities are willing to take unpleasant steps to exert control over the economy, eg to check INFLATION.

From 1932 until late in 1951, the British bank rate remained at 2 per cent, apart from a temporary increase in 1939. That is, for two decades the authorities pursued a CHEAP MONEY policy. In 1951 the rate was raised to 2½ per cent; to 5½ in 1956; and to a crisis level of 7 per cent in 1957. By 1960 it had been down to 4 per cent, and climbed again to 7 per cent in July 1961. It was down to 4 per cent by January 1963 but in November 1964 the rate was raised to 7 per cent by the Labour government in an attempt to restore confidence in sterling. By May 1967, it was down to 5½ per cent.

See also 'BACK-DOOR' OPERATIONS, OPEN MARKET OPERATIONS and SPECIAL DEPOSITS.

bank reserves. This is the amount of money banks must keep available to meet the demands of depositors. See CASH RATIO and DEPOSIT.

Bank Return. Since the BANK CHARTER ACT, 1844, the Bank of England is bound to issue a weekly statement of accounts in both the Issue and Banking Departments. This Bank Return is issued on Thursdays and the main items include Bankers' Deposits, FIDUCIARY ISSUE, government debt (see NATIONAL DEBT), and GOVERNMENT SECURITIES.

barter. The exchange of one commodity or service directly for another without the use of MONEY. The main deficiencies of barter are that a 'double coincidence of wants' is necessary; there is usually a lack of a means of subdivision; and there is no independent measure of value.

Basle Agreements. On 13th March 1961, at a normal monthly meeting of the BANK FOR INTERNATIONAL SETTLEMENTS in Basle, the representatives of the member CENTRAL BANKS discussed possible action to maintain stability in the foreign exchange rates. This discussion had become necessary because of the biggest post-war wave of speculation in currencies. In particular, there was lack of confidence in sterling, and considerable speculation against it.

This 'essay in short-term banking accommodation' assisted sterling in the next three months to the extent of £325 million.

bear. A person who sells something, eg securities, he does not possess. That is, someone who makes a 'short sale' in the anticipation of buying, before delivery is due, at a lower price. In the STOCK EXCHANGE, it would mean someone who, anticipating lower prices, sells 'for the ACCOUNT' in the hope of being able to buy at a lower price than he has sold at, before the next 'settling day'. See also BACKWARDATION, BULL and CONTANGO.

bearer security. This is a type of SECURITY the ownership of which is transferred by delivery alone.

Benelux. The Benelux Customs Union was formed in 1948 by Belgium, the Netherlands and Luxembourg. The objective of the union was to achieve full economic unity and co-operation in politics and financial and social problems. A joint external tariff and abolition of customs duties between themselves were achieved before the advent of the EUROPEAN ECONOMIC COMMUNITY, which has, of course, somewhat diminished the significance of Benelux.

bias. A SAMPLE that is not representative of its POPULATION is said to contain *bias*.

big five. The name given to the five largest CLEARING BANKS in England and Wales. They are Barclays, Lloyds, Midland, National Provincial and Westminster.

big seven. The name given to the seven largest CLEARING BANKS in England and Wales, ie the BIG FIVE plus Martins and District.

bilateral agreement. An agreement between two parties.

bilateralism. In contrast to a system of MULTILATERAL trade, bilateralism denotes a system of special trade and payments arrangements between pairs of countries.

bilateral monopoly. If a market condition should exist in which there is only one buyer of a commodity or service and only one seller of it, the state of affairs may be described as a bilateral monopoly. See BUYER'S MONOPOLY and MONOPOLY.

bill of credit. See LETTER OF CREDIT.

bill of exchange. See COMMERCIAL BILLS.

bill of lading. A document signed by the master of a ship, or his agent, as a receipt for goods (loaded on his ship), which he undertakes to deliver to the consignee. The bill is not a NEGOTIABLE INSTRUMENT, but it is, however, often used as a means of transferring the ownership of goods.

bill of sale. A document which formally transfers the right of ownership of specified goods from one person to another.

bimodal. A DISTRIBUTION is said to be bimodal when it contains two concentrations of values, ie two MODES. Generally, distributions with more than one mode are called *multimodal*.

binomial distribution. A common form of PROBABILITY DISTRIBUTION in which the events can take either of two categories, eg success or failure, heads or tails, etc. If either possibility has an equal chance of occuring then the distribution will be symmetrical, otherwise it will exhibit SKEWNESS.

bivariate. This type of DISTRIBUTION contains pairs of values of two VARIABLES. See CORRELATION and REGRESSION.

black market. A market in which all transactions violate legislation concerning rationing and prices. See also PRICE FIXING.

blocked account. When foreign holders of a country's currency, or assets expressed in terms of that currency, cannot freely use such holdings, they are said to be 'blocked'. See SECURITY STERLING and STERLING BALANCES.

blue chip. An industrial SECURITY of high quality.

Board of Trade. The government department with the general responsibility for Britain's domestic and overseas trade and for the determination of policy in certain fields, for example, concerning IMPORTS, EXPORTS and TARIFFS; negotiations and relations with international bodies and other countries; trade marks and RESALE PRICE MAINTENANCE.

bond. A document, by signing which an obligation is made to pay a specified sum in the future. It is a certificate of indebtedness, and is classed with annuities and DEBENTURES as debts owed by a government, public body or company. See also SECURITIES.

bond-washing. The practice of selling securities before the dividend (see CUM-dividend), and buying them back after the dividend has been paid (see EX-dividend). This once resulted in a 'capital gain' that was not taxable, but in Britain the Finance Acts of 1950 and 1962 dealt blows to this (see CAPITAL GAINS TAX).

bonus shares. See CAPITALISATION.

book value. If all the assets of a company were changed into cash at the values appearing in the books of the firm and all those having prior claims, eg DEBENTURE holders, were paid in full, then book value would be the proportionate amount of money that would accrue to each share of the outstanding capital.

boom. A period of expanding business activity, characterised by rapidly rising MARKET PRICES of securities and commodities, quicker TURNOVER, virtual absence of UNEMPLOYMENT, and increased PROFITS.

The opposite to a boom is a DEPRESSION. See also TRADE CYCLE.

branch banking. The typical 'commercial' bank in most countries is a very large institution with a large number of branches. For example, Britain, Canada and Australia have such a branch banking system, the British eleven London CLEARING BANKS having nearly 10,000 branches between them.

In the USA the banking system is still one of predominantly CHAIN and UNIT BANKING.

break-even point. That point in PRODUCTION at which total COSTS equal total REVENUE, where no abnormal PROFIT is received. See NORMAL PROFIT.

broker. A broker is a person who acts as a go-between in a transaction involving two or more people or institutions. There are several kinds of brokers; some deal in property, others in insurance. The term is, however, most commonly applied to STOCKBROKERS, who are members of a STOCK EXCHANGE and, as such, act as agents for the public in the buying and selling of securities. See GOVERNMENT BROKER.

brokerage. The commission that is paid to a BROKER for his services. It is usually a percentage of the amount involved in the transaction.

budget. A budget is a formal statement of estimated future income and expenditure. The British national budget is presented by the Chancellor of the EXCHEQUER to the House of Commons every year at about mid-April.

In recent years it has been the practice of the government to publish, before the budget speech, a White Paper known as the Economic Survey. This publication gives details of such things as the BALANCE OF PAYMENTS, NATIONAL INCOME, summaries of production in important industries, consumer expenditure, investment, distribution of labour, etc and compares the items with previous years. The survey often clearly indicates what remedies are needed for the economy and thus suggests how the budget might be framed.

With the great increase in government intervention in the economy that the twentieth century has seen, the budget has become more and more an instrument of policy. See DEFICIT FINANCING.

building society. A building society provides long-term loans on the security of property (see MORTGAGE) for the purchase of houses for owner-occupation. Funds are obtained from the general public, who are paid a rate of INTEREST lower than that charged to borrowers.

'built in stabiliser'. Used in most systems of TAXATION to remove automatically a smaller proportion of *total private income* (see NATIONAL INCOME) in a DEPRESSION than in a BOOM.

bull. A term used on the STOCK EXCHANGE to describe a person who buys SECURITIES in the anticipation of a rise in the market price. If he buys without the money to pay with, then he is buying 'for the ACCOUNT,' hoping to be able to sell again before the next SETTLEMENT. If he is unable to do so he will wish to *carry-over* the transaction until the next settlement (see CONTANGO). A 'tired' or 'stale' bull is one who has made a purchase and is willing to sell at no profit, or even at a loss.

See also BEAR and BACKWARDATION.

bullion. Gold or silver, usually in the form of bars or ingots of a recognised degree of purity. Bullion may be in the form of coins.

business cycle. See TRADE CYCLE.

buyers' market. A condition in a MARKET when prices are low, ie favourable to buyers. This usually means that there is an excess of SUPPLY over DEMAND and sellers are willing to accept lower prices to dispose of their goods or services. See SELLERS' MARKET and SUPPLY AND DEMAND, LAW OF.

buyer's monopoly. When there is only one buyer. A buyer's monopoly, or *monopsony*, is most likely to occur when the single buyer is a government.

by-product. A PRODUCT resulting incidentally from the manufacture of another. See JOINT SUPPLY.

call. When new securities are issued (see NEW ISSUE) it is common for the NOMINAL VALUE, or the nominal value plus a premium, to be paid in instalments or 'calls'.

capacity. The maximum amount that a FIRM can produce with a given supply of FACTORS OF PRODUCTION.

capital. The central theme of modern definitions is that capital is a 'produced means of production' or 'wealth set aside for the production of further wealth'.

Capital may be in the form of MONEY or goods (some intangible—see *personal capital* below); this is accumulated from the proceeds of past production and is used to acquire, by a process called INVESTMENT, *capital goods*, which will be used in conjunction with other factors to produce goods of a capital or consumer nature, or services.

The following is a selection of different types of capital:

authorised or nominal capital: the amount of *share capital* fixed by a company's MEMORANDUM OF ASSOCIATION;

circulating capital: either that which fulfils its function in one use, ie which is completely consumed and merged into a new product or that which must be transformed physically to be productive.;

consumer's capital: synonymous with CONSUMER GOOD;

fixed capital: that which is in durable form and can be used repeatedly; may include GOODWILL, ie intangible fixed capital;

floating, working or unspecialised capital: that which can perform more than one function, eg money,

loan capital: see DEBENTURE;

long-term capital: money invested in SECURITIES;

natural capital: LAND;

paid-up capital: the amount of *authorised capital* that has been subscribed;

personal capital: the personal skill possessed by a person as a result of training;

private capital: goods owned and producing for their owner an income;

producer's, trade or real capital: raw materials and plant used directly for production;

share capital: the capital issued by companies in the form of securities;

short-term capital: funds invested for only a short period;

social capital: either capital regarded in its social aspect when functioning as a factor of production or possessions belonging to the community for communal use (see INFRA-STRUCTURE);

specialised, sunk or specific capital: that which has only one use;

subscribed capital: 'stock' (ie securities);

uncalled capital: the amount of *share capital* not 'paid-up';

working capital: synonymous with *floating capital*. See INTEREST; also FROZEN and LIQUID.

capital consumption. The using up of CAPITAL. See DEPRECIATION.

capital expenditure. The amount paid to acquire an ASSET. See INVESTMENT.

capital formation. The making of CAPITAL, that is, the process by which money capital is accumulated (see SAVING) and converted into capital goods (see INVESTMENT). See PROPENSITY TO INVEST.

capital gains tax. A TAX that is paid upon the profit made from the buying and selling of ASSETS.

capital good. See CAPITAL.

capital-intensive product. A commodity the production of which calls for relatively more CAPITAL and relatively less LABOUR than the general average.

capitalisation issue. This is a free ISSUE of SECURITIES to those who are already shareholders, with the object of bringing a company's CAPITAL structure into line with the true value of its ASSETS. Such an issue may take place if the RESERVES of the company have swollen and it is decided to convert a proportion of them into share capital. A capitalisation issue is sometimes called a *bonus* or *scrip* issue.

capitalism. An economic system in which the means of production are wholly or substantially privately owned. See SOCIALISM.

capital levy. A tax on CAPITAL, usually of a non-recurring nature and imposed on a graduated scale according to the amount of capital owned.

capital market. A network of institutions through which the SAVINGS and surplus funds of the economy are channelled to commerce and industry, local and central government, both domestic and foreign. A capital market consists of the savers, the borrowers and the intermediaries.

capital movement. This term usually refers to the movement of *money capital* (see CAPITAL) from one country to another. See HOT MONEY.

capital-output ratio. This is the relationship between a given increase in INVESTMENT and the associated increase in output.

carrying-over, carry-over. See CONTANGO.

carrying trade. This expression generally refers to the exchanging of commodities or services by countries; the ships transporting goods are said to be engaged in the 'carrying trade'.

cartel. A combination of firms who unite to pursue a common policy in their joint interests. The elements of such a policy are fixing of prices, agreed control of the output of the cartel members and marketing arrangements such as the division of home and export markets between members. The cartel is, therefore, a central selling organisation.
See also MARKETING BOARDS.

cash. For an individual, cash would be actual coins and bank notes in his possession; he may regard his current bank account as cash although the CHEQUE is not LEGAL TENDER. A BANK regards notes and coin in till and vaults and its balances at the CENTRAL BANK as cash. In certain circumstances, however, the monetary authorities may prevent a bank from freely drawing upon such a balance (see SPECIAL DEPOSITS). See also CURRENCY.

cash ratio. The ratio of the BANK RESERVES of cash to the volume of DEPOSITS is called the cash ratio. There is no legal requirement (as in other countries) for such a ratio, but in Britain it was maintained by the CLEARING BANKS for a long time at 10 per cent; in the years since the second world war 8 per cent has been considered adequate, part being in the till and part at the BANK OF ENGLAND.

census. A census is an official enumeration of some description, usually of DISTRIBUTION, PRODUCTION and population. See POPULATION and below.

census of distribution. See below.

census of population. The official counting of the population of a specified area and the obtaining of information concerning age, marital status, number of children, occupation, etc.

In Britain, a census of population is carried out every ten years. During the last, in 1961, information was also collected concerning business premises. This part of the enquiry was called the census of distribution. In 1966 a 'partial census' of population was carried out.

census of production. A periodical investigation of the production carried on by the producing units of an economy. In Britain a census of production is carried out annually and businesses employing more than ten workers must submit information. This census provides information that is valuable in the computation of NATIONAL INCOME.

central bank. A bank occupying a central position in the banking system of a country in the sense that it functions as banker to the government and to the other banks; as the manager of the currency and credit policy of the country; and as the controller of the importation and exportation of money or precious metals. Most central banks are now state-owned, as in France and Britain; those that are not are invariably under government supervision. See BANK OF ENGLAND.

central limit theorem. This states that the total of a large number of independent RANDOM VARIABLES will approximate to a NORMAL CURVE.

central tendency. A measure of this, viz an *average*, is a single numerical statement of the general magnitude of all the values in a DISTRIBUTION. It reflects the tendency of the data to concentrate at certain central values. See ARITHMETIC MEAN, DISPERSION, GEOMETRIC MEAN, HARMONIC MEAN, MEDIAN, MODE and QUADRATIC MEAN.

chain banking. When a group of banks is under substantially common ownership and control, perhaps as a result of INTERLOCKING DIRECTORATES or majority shareholding, the state of affairs is called chain or group banking.

See UNIT BANKING.

charter party. A document signed by the owner of a ship and a merchant (the charter) as a contract that the goods will be conveyed to a specified place for a specified sum.

cheap money. This term is sometimes used to describe MONEY, the value (ie purhcasing power) of which is low. It is also used to indicate any low interest rate in particular or the interest rate structure of an economy that is kept deliberately low by policy. That is, at a level lower than it would be if there were no such policy.

In Britain a 'cheap money policy' was adhered to between 1932 and 1951, during which time the BANK RATE was maintained at 2 per cent, apart from a short period in the autumn of 1939.

cheque. A written order to a banker to pay the person bearing it, or a person or body named on it, a specified sum of MONEY. A cheque is not LEGAL TENDER and a creditor can, therefore, refuse payment by one. If the cheque is 'open', that is, does not have two lines drawn parallel across its face, the banker will pay cash to the person presenting the cheque. If the cheque is 'crossed' with the two lines mentioned above, then the appropriate amount will be paid into the person's account, ie the payment will be effected by book-entries. We say that the payment has been made using BANK MONEY.

The legal definition of a cheque is 'a bill of exchange drawn on a banker payable on demand'.

See COMMERCIAL BILLS.

CIF. A contract in which the payment for the goods includes the cost of insurance and freight. See FAS, FOB and FOR.

circulating capital. See CAPITAL.

City. This is the name given to a geographically concentrated group of financial institutions in London: the BANK OF ENG-LAND, COMMERCIAL and MERCHANT BANKS, DISCOUNT HOUSES, FOREIGN EXCHANGE market, STOCK EXCHANGE, etc. The City provides a wide range of financial services and is an important exporter of INVISIBLES.

clearing banks. In Britain there are eleven clearing banks; they are called London Clearing Banks and are each members of the LONDON BANKERS' CLEARING HOUSE. In addition to the BIG SEVEN they include Coutts, Glyn Mills, National, and William Deacons. See also BANKERS' CLEARINGS.

clearing house. An institution established by a group of BANKS at which CHEQUES and other forms of commercial paper (eg COMMERCIAL BILLS) are exchanged, the balances outstanding being paid in CASH. See BANKERS' CLEARINGS, CLEARING BANKS, EUROPEAN PAYMENTS UNION and LONDON BANK-ERS' CLEARING HOUSE.

closed shop. A business in which only members of a TRADE UNION will be accepted for employment. When open to non-union members the term used is *open shop*.

closing price. At the end of the day's business in the STOCK EXCHANGE the prices then ruling are called the closing prices.

Any movements that take place afterwards are called 'after the close'.

Club of Ten. See INTERNATIONAL MONETARY FUND.

coefficients. A coefficient is an expression of a mathematical relationship. Significant coefficents in economics are those relating to the ACCELERATOR and ELASTICITY of DEMAND and SUPPLY.

coin. A form of MONEY, invariably made of metal, in a standardised and easily recognisable shape. The metal may be precious; if not, the coin is said to be TOKEN MONEY. See TOKEN COINS.

collateral security. Property, perhaps in the form of deeds to a house or stocks and shares, deposited with a creditor to guarantee that a loan will be repaid. It is customary, for example, to deposit collateral with a bank when an OVERDRAFT has been agreed to.

collective bargaining The existence of TRADE UNIONS and EMPLOYERS' ASSOCIATIONS makes it easier for both sides in a dispute to meet and bargain for changes in wages, hours of work, working conditions, etc. Thus the bargaining is done collectively, by representatives of both sides.

See also ARBITRATION, CONCILIATION, INDUSTRIAL COURT, JOINT INDUSTRIAL COUNCILS, etc.

combination in restraint of trade. An agreement to restrict COMPETITION. Such an agreement may create a CARTEL or HOLDING COMPANY, or devices known collectively as RESTRICTIVE TRADE PRACTICES. See also MONOPOLY.

combine. The result of AMALGAMATION, INTEGRATION and MERGER.

coming-out price. When a NEW ISSUE is made, the price at which the new securities are offered is sometimes referred to as the coming-out price.

commerce. The buying and selling, or bartering, of goods and services, particularly on a large scale.

commercial bank. In Britain, this term is largely synonymous with the CLEARING BANKS.

commercial bill. A commercial bill is a written instruction by the person drawing it (the drawer) to another (the drawee) to pay a particular sum either to the bearer of the bill or to the order of a specified person (the payee). Or, as defined in the Bills of Exchange Act, 1882, 'an unconditional order in writing addressed by one person to another, signed by the person giving it, requiring the person to whom it is addressed to pay on demand or at a fixed or determinable future time a sum certain in money to or to the order of a specified person, or to bearer'.

In the British CAPITAL MARKET the commercial bill is still an important means of raising money and the total of such bills outstanding at any one time is likely to be over £700 million, evenly divided into the two main types, *bank bills* and *trade bills*.

Bank bill: a bill that has been accepted by a bank; one that is likely to have been held for most of its existence within the banking system. A bank bill can be compared with an *advance* as a method of bank lending.

Trade bill: most of these are held outside the banking system and will have been accepted by traders. They can be compared with *trade credit* as a means of borrowing and lending between businesses.

See also FOREIGN BILLS, INLAND BILLS, PROMISSORY NOTES and TREASURY BILLS.

commission. The payment, usually as a percentage of the amount involved, to an agent (eg a STOCKBROKER) for conducting a transaction. A commission may be a body with the power to act.

Committee on the Working of the Monetary System. See RADCLIFFE REPORT.

commodity. Any material thing possessing UTILITY and exchange value that is directly consumable. See ECONOMIC GOOD and SERVICE.

commodity market. See LONDON COMMODITY EXCHANGE.

commodity money. A form of MONEY possessing the qualities of a COMMODITY.

common market. An arrangement, usually between countries, whereby trade restrictions between the members are abolished and a common external tariff policy is adopted. It is possible that the co-operation may extend into social and political fields as well.

In Europe, the establishment of BENELUX and the EUROPEAN COAL AND STEEL COMMUNITY was followed in 1957 by the more comprehensive EUROPEAN ECONOMIC COMMUNITY, which has come to be known as the 'Common Market', although its implications are far wider than a CUSTOMS UNION.

Commonwealth Development Corporation. The name given in 1963 to the Colonial Development Corporation, which had been established in 1948 to help the economic development of British dependent territories.

communism. A political theory that the ownership of all WEALTH, ie the means of production, exchange and distribution, should be vested in the community as a whole. This would mean the virtual abolition of private property, that individuals would contribute according to their ability and would consume according to their needs.

company. Under British law, companies may be either private or public, ie may be either a *private limited company* or a *public joint-stock company*. The former may have between two and fifty shareholders; the latter from seven upwards, with no maximum. In a private company a shareholder cannot transfer shares without the consent of the company and no invitation can be made to the general public to subscribe for shares. In a public company, the objects of its activities, and its powers, must be set out in the MEMORANDUM OF ASSOCIATION, which must also contain the name (ending in 'limited') and address of the company, a statement that there is LIMITED LIABILITY for the shareholders, the amount of authorised capital (see CAPITAL) and the kinds of SECURITIES to be issued.

Both types of companies must be registered with the Registrar of Companies. After registration the public company can issue a PROSPECTUS offering securities to the public.

Companies have been strictly regulated by the Companies Acts of 1869, 1929 and 1948, the main objective of which has been to protect the public from fraudulent activities.

See also ARTICLES OF ASSOCIATION, HOLDING COMPANY, JOINT STOCK and SUBSIDIARY COMPANY.

company promoter. A person who assumes responsibility for the launching of a COMPANY. In particular, he may undertake to raise the necessary CAPITAL by selling SECURITIES. See ISSUING HOUSE, etc.

company tax. See TAXATION.

comparative advantages. This principle is usually applied to international trade, but is essentially an extension of DIVISION OF LABOUR, ie SPECIALISATION.

The theory states that a country will tend to specialise in the production of those commodities for which it is best fitted and in which it has the greatest comparative advantage (ie lowest comparative cost). If, for example, country A can produce two commodities X and Y cheaper than country B, but its advantage is greater with X than with Y, then it will gain by concentrating production on X rather than Y. FREE TRADE is assumed in the theory, which might also be expressed as follows: a country will gain by specialising in the production of those commodities in which its *comparative cost* advantage is greater, exporting these commodities and importing commodities in which its comparative cost advantage is less.

competition. A MARKET condition in which there is an indeterminate number of buyers and sellers, each intent on maximising PROFIT or satisfaction and in which PRICE is subject to control only by the forces of SUPPLY and DEMAND. This condition, in which no single trade can exert influence, is sometimes called *free competition*, and approximates to PERFECT COMPETITION. See also DUOPOLY, IMPERFECT COMPETITION, MONOPOLY and OLIGOPOLY.

composite demand. The aggregate DEMAND for a commodity or service deriving from a variety of wants, each being satisfied by the commodity or service, eg the demand for unskilled workers.

composite supply. Whenever a particular want can be satisfied in a variety of ways, the aggregate of this variety is the *composite supply*, for example, the need for entertainment or transport can be satisfied in a number of different ways. See SUPPLY.

compound interest. INTEREST that is calculated upon the original sum invested or lent plus accumulated interest. See SIMPLE INTEREST.

Comprehensive Development Areas. In 1948, local authorities were given power to declare substantial worn-out areas of city property as Comprehensive Development Areas. Once declared, the authorities could compulsorily buy the land for wholesale, rather than piecemeal, development.
See SPECIAL AREAS and DEVELOPMENT AREAS.

conciliation. The act of bringing two parties together in an attempt to find a peaceful way out of a difficulty. In the case of a dispute between employers and employees it is in the interest of the public and the disputants themselves that all possible methods of reaching a settlement should be tried, if, for example, a STRIKE or LOCK-OUT has been threatened.
See also INDUSTRIAL COURT and JOINT INDUSTRIAL COUNCILS.

Confederation of British Industry. An organisation representing British employers formed in 1964 by an amalgamation of the British Employers' confederation, Federation of British Industries and the National Union of Manufacturers.

confidence interval. The numerical limits, usually stated in PROBABILITY terms, within which the statistician expects a PARAMETER to fall.

Consolidated Fund Services. That part of British government expenditure established by permanent statutes, such as the charges on the NATIONAL DEBT, the Sovereign's Civil List and a number of special salaries, annuities and pensions, including part of the expenses of the Courts of Justice.

Consols. This is an abbreviation for Consolidated Annuities, which are funded GOVERNMENT SECURITIES (see also FUNDED DEBT), ie the government need not repay them until it wishes.

Consols are, in fact, irredeemable (see REDEEMABLE) 2½ per cent securities issued by the British government in 1921 or after.

consumer. The person for whom CONSUMER GOODS have UTILITY; ie have the ability to satisfy a want.

consumer durable. A long-lasting CONSUMER GOOD. This might also be called *consumption capital* (see CAPITAL).

consumer good. Something used for the direct satisfaction of human wants; it may be short- or long-lived (see CONSUMER DURABLE). The expression is used to distinguish those goods which are not capital goods (see CAPITAL); the distinction being one of usage. In fact, a single commodity can act as either; for example, coal can be used in the home for the production of heat which is directly consumed or it can be used by a manufacturer to produce steam power or as a raw material, ie in a capital sense. Consumer and capital goods together constitute ECONOMIC GOODS.

consumer's capital. This is synonymous with CONSUMER GOOD. See also CAPITAL.

consumer's sovereignty. The belief that the CONSUMER is the supreme ruler of the economy because of his control of the MARKET. This conception is based upon the forces of DEMAND in the market, ie if price is low, consumers will demand more and PRODUCERS will be encouraged to produce more; if price is higher than consumers are prepared to pay, the demand falls, price falls, and producers are discouraged.
The conception is, of course, naïve. It does not, for example, take account of production in anticipation of demand and the subsequent creation of a demand, say, through advertising; nor of RESTRICTIVE TRADE PRACTICES.

consumer's surplus. The difference between what a CONSUMER actually pays for a commodity or service and the maximum amount he would be prepared to pay. Thus, 'surplus' is a measure of the extra monetary sacrifices a person would have been willing to make to acquire something.
A certain amount of UTILITY has, therefore, been obtained for no outlay.

consumption. The act of using CONSUMER GOODS, that is, the using up of UTILITY. The term is sometimes used to describe the using up of all ECONOMIC GOODS, ie consumer goods and capital goods (see CAPITAL); the latter being consumed to produce other goods and, perhaps, called producers' goods or production goods.
See INDUCED CONSUMPTION.

contango. The STOCK EXCHANGE technique whereby a buyer has bought SECURITIES, but wishes to defer payment for them from one SETTLEMENT DAY (see ACCOUNT) to the next. The BULL, or 'giver', is allowed to 'contango' upon payment of a rate of interest, upon the sum involved, to the BEAR (the 'taker' or deliverer of the securities).

The technique is also called *carry-over*, *carrying-over*, *continuation* and *give-on* and the word contango is sometimes applied to the rate of interest involved.

See also BACKWARDATION and TAKE-IN.

continuation. See CONTANGO.

continuous. When a VARIABLE can assume any value within a numerical range, ie when it is measured to the nearest millimetre, 0·001, ounce, etc, the resulting data is said to be *continuous*.

contract. A legally binding agreement, the terms of which may be oral, written or implied.

conventional necessities. Those CONSUMER GOODS not strictly necessary for subsistence, but regarded as necessities because, from custom, it is normal to have them. Adam Smith recognised them and said that 'custom renders it indecent to live without them'.

conversion. The substitution of a loan at a given rate by one at a lower rate of interest. Holders of the SECURITY in question are usually given the option of 'converting' their holdings into the new loan or of being paid off in cash. A 'conversion issue' may, therefore, be described as one of refinancing a maturing issue.

convertibility. Originally, this term referred to a currency which could be freely exchanged for gold at a fixed price, ie the currency was 'convertible'. Thus, if a country was on a full GOLD STANDARD, any holders of that country's currency could freely convert it into gold or any other currency.

In recent years, after the widespread abandonment of gold standards and the exigencies of EXCHANGE CONTROL, the term convertibility has come to apply to foreign holders of the domestic currency. If a currency possesses convertibility, foreign earners of that currency can convert their holdings of it into gold or any other currency.

Co-operative Societies. These may be divided, broadly, into two categories: *consumers'* and *producers'*.

Consumers': The consumer co-operative movement in Britain dates from 1844 and may be described as associations of consumers engaged in the retail trade, sharing out the profits as a 'dividend' among the members. It began in Rochdale, when a group of weavers opened a shop in order to prevent the exploitation of working people by unscrupulous employers who had opened their own 'tommy' shops from which their workers were obliged to buy. After the first world war, the movement grew rapidly, and by the middle of the century well over a thousand societies were in existence, with 12 million members.

Another line of development began when a number of retail societies combined to engage in some of the simpler forms of production, eg bread-making. In the 1860s the English and Scottish Co-operative Wholesale Societies were formed to produce on a large scale and distribute their products to the retail co-operative stores. The wholesale societies have a similar relationship with the retail ones, as do the latter ones with their members. The profits of the CWS are shared out among the retail societies according to their purchases from it. The Co-operative Wholesale Society is engaged in many forms of production, including tea plantations, the manufacture of clothing and the operation of a bank.

Producers': these co-operative societies are associations of producers to co-operate in production and marketing and to share the trading profits between members. In Britain they have met with little success and it is only in the boot and shoe, printing and textile trades that they have been continually successful. Co-operation between British farmers has steadily gained ground, but in other European countries it has long been firmly established in agriculture, eg in Ireland and Denmark, and other industries.

corner. The concentration of the total or major part of the supply of any ECONOMIC GOOD in the possession of one or more persons, with the object of raising the market price by the artificial scarcity created.

correlation. The relationship which exists when two VARIABLES vary one with the other; that is, when large values of one correspond with large values of the other (*direct* or *positive* correlation), or large values of one correspond with low values of the other (*inverse* or *negative* correlation). See REGRESSION.

Cost of Living Index. See Index of Retail Prices under INDEX NUMBER.

Cost of Production Theory of Value. This theory developed out of the LABOUR THEORY OF VALUE and states that the value of a good or service depends upon the cost of all the FACTORS OF PRODUCTION employed to make it.

cost, prime and total. See COSTS.

cost-push. See INFLATION.

costs. This term can be discussed in both monetary and non-monetary senses. In general, we say that costs are involved whenever a commodity or a service is produced; so that when the owner of a FACTOR OF PRODUCTION offers its services to a producer the cost to the owner is one of direct CONSUMPTION foregone; whereas, for the producer, there is a definite, measurable, monetary cost involved in the employment of the services of the factor in the productive process. It is customary to give the latter type of cost a name, eg wages, salaries, rent, interest.

The basic division is into those incurred before actual production is possible—and when it has stopped—and those which vary according to the volume of production (within a fixed capacity). The first may be called *fixed*, *overhead*, *supplementary* or *sunk* and are regular, established, unavoidable charges whether *fixed assets* (see ASSET) are being used or not, eg taxes, rents (in the commercial sense), interest, insurance, maintenance and depreciation charges, reserves, certain salaries, etc. The second are usually called *prime*, *operating running* or *variable* and consist of payments for materials to be used in production, for power and for the labour to be employed. These costs, therefore, increase as production increases and will only be constant when production is constant.

At any time, even when production is nil, there will be a *total cost*, consisting of fixed and variable costs (the latter may be nil when production is nil). Theoretically, it should be possible to ascertain the actual cost of producing any particular unit of output; this could be called *unit cost*. The addition to total cost involved in producing one more unit of output is then the *marginal cost*.

coupon. A certificate entitling the possessor to the payment of interest or dividend on a certain security, normally of the BEARER type.

cover. This can refer to security for a loan (see COLLATERAL SECURITY), to insurance against risk (see HEDGING) and to the number of times a COMPANY'S dividends are covered by its earnings.

craft union. A craft union is a TRADE UNION with a membership confined to workers in one or a small number of skilled trades This type of union is sometimes called *horizontal* because it cuts across the industrial structure of an economy. Examples are to be found in Britain in the woodworking and engineering trades.

See also INDUSTRIAL UNION.

credit. In general, this means the granting of a period of time by a creditor to a debtor at the expiration of which the latter must pay the debt. In book-keeping it means the acknowledgement of payment by a book-entry. See BANK CREDIT and VOLUME OF CREDIT.

credit base. This term is sometimes used instead of CASH RATIO, ie it consists of the accounts of COMMERCIAL BANKS at the CENTRAL BANK, plus the CASH in their tills, which together make up the base on which a certain VOLUME OF CREDIT is created; the ratio of the 'base' to the superstructure of credit having been established by custom or law.

In Britain today, however, the credit base, so far as the CLEARING BANKS are concerned, is the LIQUIDITY RATIO.

See also OPEN MARKET OPERATIONS and SPECIAL DEPOSITS.

credit card. Early in 1966, a number of British banks launched schemes known variously as bankers' card, cheque card, credit card, etc. The first two are similar: a card issued to customers guarenteeing the holder's cheques up to £30. The purpose is to enable a customer to withdraw cash from a number of the offices of the participating banks. It was hoped that the credit card would also make easier the acceptance of cheques by shops, hotels, etc.

credit control. Any policy, governmental or otherwise, designed to exercise control over the VOLUME OF CREDIT, ie to keep it constant, contract or expand it. See BANK RATE, OPEN MARKET OPERATIONS and SPECIAL DEPOSITS.

credit money. This term is sometimes used to mean FIDUCIARY ISSUE, but may refer to forms of MONEY also called 'credit instruments', eg CHEQUES, and COMMERCIAL BILLS.

credit sale. See HIRE PURCHASE.

Credit Theory of the Trade Cycle. The theory that the TRADE CYCLE, the cyclical expansion and contraction of economic activity, is mainly the result of increases and decreases in the VOLUME OF CREDIT.

credit transfer. In the 1950s, there was a large expansion in HIRE PURCHASE spending, regular saving and investment, home ownership, etc, all of which required the making of regular payments. The increased need for a new and simple means of settling debts led to the introduction, in March 1961, of the *bank credit transfer scheme*. Under this scheme, it is possible for anyone, whether a bank customer or not, to pay a bill through any of the 12,000 or so branches of the eleven London CLEARING BANKS and the Scottish Banks without having to make out a cheque. In the case of a non-customer, he must call at one of the above branches, fill in the appropriate form, and pay across the counter the amount (plus a charge of 6d) he wishes credited to someone's account in any other branch or bank.

See also GIRO.

cum-. A prefix meaning 'with' that is much used in finance. The main terms with which the prefix is used are shown on the following page.

cum-bonus means that the price paid for SECURITIES secures, in addition, the right to a bonus issue (see CAPITALISATION);

cum-dividend means that the new possessor of securities receives the DIVIDEND that has accrued since the last distribution (this may be abbreviated to *cum-div*);

cum-interest means the same as *cum-dividend*, but the new owner receives the current interest, not the accrued dividend;

cum-rights means that the buyer has paid a price that includes the right to any benefit recently conferred, eg a RIGHTS ISSUE. See also EX-.

cumulative dividend. See ACCUMULATIVE DIVIDEND.

cumulative frequency distribution. This is a development of the frequency DISTRIBUTION in which the frequencies are accumulated from one end to the other. The graphical presentation is often called an *ogive*.

cumulative preference securities. See SECURITIES.

currency. Anything which is acceptable as a *medium of exchange*, that is, as MONEY, can be called currency. It does not have to be LEGAL TENDER. although the term is frequently used to exclude other forms of money, eg CHEQUES and postal orders.

currency depreciation. See DEPRECIATION.

current account. See DEPOSIT.

current asset. See ASSET.

customs duty. A tax levied on commodities transported from one country to another, ie on IMPORTS and/or EXPORTS. It is more usual for this kind of TARIFF to be imposed on imports. See AD VALOREM DUTY, EXCISE DUTY, PROTECTION, and TAXATION.

customs union. An agreement established by two or more countries whereby the signatories eliminate all TARIFFS, CUSTOMS DUTIES and quantitative restrictions (see QUOTAS) existing between them. The members also adopt a common tariff policy regarding trade with non-member countries. A customs union is sometimes called a *tariff union*. See COMMON MARKET, BENELUX, EUROPEAN COAL AND STEEL COMMUNITY, EUROPEAN ECONOMIC COMMUNITY and ZOLLVEREIN.

cybernetics. The science of control and communication processes in animals and machines.

dear money. This term is commonly used to refer to a period of high interest rates, but it is sometimes used when MONEY has a high purchasing power, ie when the level of prices is low. See CHEAP MONEY and BANK RATE.

death duties. TAXATION levied upon the estate of a deceased person. It may take either of two forms: (*a*) when the gross value of the estate is assessed and taxed before it is divided up between the beneficiaries; and, (b) when what is received by the beneficiaries is taxed. The former is usually called an *estate duty*; the latter type may be called an *inheritance, legacy, or succession tax*. It is normal for all to be imposed in a progressive way, ie at a rate which increases as the amount to be taxed increases.

debenture. A debenture has been defined as 'a document which either creates a debt or acknowledges it'. A debenture does not necessarily confer any special rights or privileges upon the holder, although it is usually secured in some way, and is repayable within a specified time. It is customary for a debenture to bear a fixed rate of interest, which must be paid whether or not the borrower makes a profit. The borrower is usually a COMPANY, so that the debentures may be called *loan capital*, secured on specific ASSETS of the *company*.
See PERPETUAL DEBENTURE and SECURITIES.

debit. A book-keeping entry recording an amount owing. See CREDIT.

debt. Something owed by one person, or body, to another. See FLOATING DEBT, FUNDED DEBT and NATIONAL DEBT.

debt service. The payment of interest on a DEBT, plus whatever instalments of the PRINCIPAL are due. The term is most commonly used in connection with the NATIONAL DEBT.

debts, public. See NATIONAL DEBT.

decentralisation. A term usually applied to the practice of establishing INDUSTRY away from urban areas and, perhaps, away from other industries.

decile. The nine PERCENTILE points which divide a DISTRIBUTION into ten parts are the deciles. For example, the fifth decile is the MEDIAN.

decimal currency. A CURRENCY based on the decimal system, ie multiples and parts of ten. An official enquiry (Committee of Enquiry on Decimal Currency) into the decimalisation of the British system reported in 1963. Its majority recommendation advocated division of the £ into 100 units equivalent to 2·4d each. It was announced in 1966 that Britain would adopt a decimal currency in 1971.

deferred demand. A DEMAND that has to be postponed because of the scarcity of a commodity or service.

deferred income. See UNEARNED INCOME.

deferred securities. SECURITIES that rank for DIVIDEND only after other forms have been satisfied, ie after DEBENTURE holders and *preference* and *ordinary shareholders* have been paid.

deficit. A deficiency in monetary terms. It usually refers to the amount by which liabilities exceed ASSETS, or expenditure exceeds revenue. See DEFICIT FINANCING.

deficit financing. This refers to the attempt to alleviate a DEPRESSION by the deliberate spending, by the state, of more than it received in revenue. This spending will usually be on public works of some kind, so that the state, as an employer, will increase the purchasing power of the community and generate economic activity. The deficit in the national BUDGET can be met by borrowing, or by the printing of more money.

In the USA, the term *pump-priming* is frequently used.

deflation. When the supply of MONEY falls relative to the number of exchange transactions, prices fall and a deflation exists. That is, incomes have been reduced or are not being spent and the amount of goods and services offered has not contracted to the same extent, with the result that the price level falls.

See also REFLATION and QUANTITY THEORY OF MONEY.

deflationary gap. In a DEFLATION all the goods and services available are not being absorbed because of a deficiency in spending. The volume of spending, either privately or by the government, needed to bring the total volume up to a level at which all goods and services are being absorbed, is the 'deflationary gap'.

degrees of freedom. A mathematical concept which makes use of the number of observations from which a statistic is computed to identify which THEORETICAL DISTRIBUTION should be applied to a problem.

demand. The demand for an ECONOMIC GOOD at any time is the amount of it that will be bought at a given price. At different prices it is likely that different amounts will be bought.

If an individual, group of individuals, or an institution desire to possess a good, but do not have the means to acquire it, this is not demand in the economic sense. For the economist, demand is always *effective demand*, ie the desire to buy must be coupled with the ability to pay.

See ALTERNATE DEMAND, COMPOSITE DEMAND, DE-FERRED DEMAND, DERIVED DEMAND, ELASTICITY OF DEMAND, JOINT DEMAND and POTENTIAL DEMAND.

demand-pull. See INFLATION.

Departmental Joint Council. During 1919 and 1920 the British government, as an employer of considerable numbers of industrial workers, took steps to apply the principles of the Whitley Report (see WHITLEY COMMITTEE) to government industrial establishments. Departmental and TRADE JOINT COUNCILS were set up. The former consider and discuss matters other than trade questions domestic to the department concerned.

Department of Economic Affairs. The Labour government formed after the general election of 15th October 1964 contained the new post of Minister for Economic Affairs. It was stated that his department would be 'responsible for framing and supervising the plan for economic development and for the general co-ordination of action to implement the plan and also for all economic policy related to industrial expansion, allocation of physical resources and regional implications of the expansion programme'. The new department thus took over some of the functions of the BOARD OF TRADE, the NATIONAL ECONOMIC DEVELOPMENT COUNCIL and the TREASURY.

deposit. When MONEY is placed in a BANK (or, for example, BUILDING SOCIETY) it is said to be 'deposited'. The money may be put into an account from which it can be drawn at any time, or into an account which can only be drawn upon after certain notice has been given. In British banking, these types of accounts are known as *current accounts* and *deposit accounts* respectively and the latter is usually the only one to command interest payments. In the USA, the corresponding terms are 'demand deposits' and 'time (or notice) deposits'. The terms *cash deposits* and *savings deposits* are sometimes used to denote those being continually turned over in the settlements of debts and those not held for current business, but as INVESTMENTS or SAVINGS. The term *bank deposits* embraces all the above, referring to the entries in books of banks showing that persons, corporations and others have a claim against the bank.

It is most important to note that a banker can create bank deposits by giving a person or corporation a claim against him, not in return for money deposited, but for COLLATERAL SECURITY deposited with him, ie he makes an advance and thus creates additional BANK MONEY. He also creates a deposit when he buys SECURITIES from the public. See also BANK RESERVES and CASH RATIO.

depreciation. This term is used in economics to refer to the fall in value of something; it is used mainly in connection with CAPITAL and CURRENCY.

In the first sense it means the using up of *capital goods*, or *capital consumption*. The fall in value may come from wear and tear or obsolescence or corrosion, etc. All businesses properly run make allowances for depreciation by deciding how long an ASSET will last, ie by establishing a 'rate of depreciation' and then proceed to set aside funds which will accumulate into an amount large enough to replace the asset when the time comes to 'write it off'.

Depreciation of currency refers to the reduced purchasing power of MONEY, which may be the result of an increase in the supply of money. When the value of a currency in terms of other currencies falls, it is said to have 'depreciated'. The prices of that country's goods to foreign buyers fall, accordingly, and this may lead to an increase in exports.

See also DEVALUATION.

Depressed Areas. A general term, like *distressed areas*, used to refer to those parts of Britain containing the staple industries (coal, iron and steel, shipbuilding, etc) which were 'depressed' for most of the years between the two world wars. See also COMPREHENSIVE DEVELOPMENT AREAS, DEVELOPMENT AREAS, SPECIAL AREAS and UNEMPLOYMENT.

depression. This is one of the two names (the other being *slump*) given to a period in which business activity is at a low ebb; prices and wages are low; there is a high level of UNEMPLOYMENT (cyclical unemployment); little borrowing from the banks; and a general feeling of pessimism amongst businessmen. In other words, it is the lowest phase of the TRADE CYCLE. See also BOOM, RECESSION and REVIVAL.

derived demand. The DEMAND for an ECONOMIC GOOD that arises out of the wish to satisfy the demand for another commodity or service. The demand for a building, for example, will create demands for cement, bricks, timber, etc, all of which are derived demands.

devaluation. A downward change in the valuation of one CURRENCY in terms of others. In a free FOREIGN EXCHANGE market such a downward movement would normally be called DEPRECIATION; but when not free, and EXCHANGE RATES are imposed by the monetary authorities, the movement would be deliberate and called devaluation.

The opposite of devaluation is REVALUATION.

Development Areas. The measures taken by the British government in the years between the two world wars to assist areas suffering from prolonged DEPRESSION (see DEPRESSED AREAS and SPECIAL AREAS), were reinforced in 1945 by the passing of the Distribution of Industry Act. This Act, like the pre-war legislation, provided for assistance to those parts of the country where there was a likelihood of a 'special danger of unemployment'.

In 1960, the Local Unemployment Act virtually did away with the category of Development Areas by empowering the government to give the assistance, formerly only available to the areas, to any district (see DEVELOPMENT DISTRICTS) vulnerable to unemployment.

See also COMPREHENSIVE DEVELOPMENT AREAS.

Development Districts. The Local Unemployment Act of 1960 abandoned the old notion of DEVELOPMENT AREAS and substituted Development Districts, to be designated by the BOARD OF TRADE from time to time.

differential duty. See DISCRIMINATORY DUTY.

diminishing productivity. In the theory of economics, one of the fundamental 'laws' postulates that when FACTORS OF PRODUCTION are interacting productively and the amount of one or more of those factors is fixed, then the application of further increments of the other, variable, factor or factors will, at some time, yield diminishing increases in production. It is said that there is *diminishing productivity*, or *diminishing returns*.

See LAW OF DIMINISHING RETURNS, MARGIN, MARGINAL PRODUCT, etc.

direct production. See ROUNDABOUT PRODUCTION.

direct taxation. See TAXATION.

discommodity. A term infrequently used to denote the opposite of a COMMODITY, ie something that does not possess UTILITY. In other words, any material thing possessing DISUTILITY.

discount. A discount is a deduction from a debt, or a price, or from the face value of something in consideration of prompt or early payment. It is used in several senses.

In the retail trade it refers to the abatement of price, usually to a particular class of customer, eg to wholesale customers (*trade discount*), or to cash-paying customers (*cash discount*).

In dealings in SECURITIES, when the price at which they are being bought and sold is less than their face value (ie falling short of PAR), the difference is said to be a discount; and in the COMMERCIAL BILL field, it is the sum deducted from the face value of the bill in consideration of the money being advanced before its date of MATURITY.

See also DISCOUNT HOUSE and DISCOUNT MARKET.

discount house. In Britain, there are two distinct types of discount house; one long established, the other a recent adoption of a practice common in the USA.

The latter is often called a *commercial credit company* in North America and is an establishment in which it is possible to obtain CONSUMER GOODS, particularly CONSUMER DURABLES, at DISCOUNTS of up to 40 per cent on normal retail prices.

The other discount houses are financial firms who lend to the government (by holding TREASURY BILLS and short-dated government BONDS) and to the private sector of the economy by holding COMMERCIAL BILLS.

See 'BACK-DOOR' OPERATIONS, BANK OF ENGLAND, BANK RATE, CASH RATIO, DISCOUNT MARKET and MONEY AT CALL.

discount market. The London Discount Market consists of twelve major DISCOUNT HOUSES and a similar number of smaller firms undertaking some of the dealings in COMMERCIAL and TREASURY BILLS and short-term GOVERNMENT SECURITIES.

discrete. This type of data can only be expressed in whole numbers (integers), eg size of family. See CONTINUOUS.

discriminatory duty. When a different duty is imposed on identical commodities depending upon the source of the import it is said to be a *differential, discriminatory* or *preferential* one. Such duties have been virtually abolished by the application of MOST-FAVOURED-NATION CLAUSES. See CUSTOMS DUTY and GENERAL AGREEMENT ON TARIFFS AND TRADE.

diseconomies of scale. See LARGE-SCALE PRODUCTION.

disintegration. See INTEGRATION.

disinvestment. A reduction in a stock of capital goods (see CAPITAL) may be called *disinvestment*. This may occur when producers do not renew worn-out capital or when capital goods are sold.

dispersion. In addition to the measures of CENTRAL TENDENCY it is necessary to know how data in a DISTRIBUTION are spread out, ie their *variability*. See MEAN DEVIATION, RANGE, SEMI-INTERQUARTILE RANGE and STANDARD DEVIATION.

dissaving. Whenever expenditure exceeds income, *dissaving* may be said to exist. Clearly, it can only continue when borrowing or realisation of CAPITAL is resorted to.

distressed areas. See DEPRESSED AREAS.

distribution. The main sense in which the economist uses this term is the apportionment of the NATIONAL INCOME among the FACTORS OF PRODUCTION which co-operate to produce that income. The *distribution* is then into INTEREST, PROFIT, RENT, and WAGES, and a theory of distribution can be evolved to account for the actual apportionments in an economy. This is sometimes called the *functional distribution*. It does not deal with what people actually receive as their shares of the national income, ie the *personal distribution*.
  Distribution is also used to refer to that part of COMMERCE responsible for the channelling of goods from producers to consumers (see RETAIL and WHOLESALER).
  In statistics, a distribution is data classified in some way, usually in a *frequency distribution*, which is an arrangement of data showing the frequency with which values occur in certain pre-determined classes or groups, eg income groups. A *frequency*

table is the tabular presentation of a frequency distribution and a *frequency chart* is a diagrammatic presentation.

disutility. When an ECONOMIC GOOD yields dissatisfaction it is said to possess negative UTILITY or *disutility*. See DISCOMMODITY.

diversification. There are several kinds of diversification: of the industries in an economy; of the industries in an area of an economy; of the activities of a particular company; and of investment (see INVESTMENT TRUST and UNIT TRUST).

dividend. A distribution from profits payable at a fixed rate on preference shares (see SECURITIES), or at a varying rate, according to the size of the profits, on ordinary shares. By the Companies Act of 1948, dividends can be paid only out of profits, unless Section 65 of the Act is satisfied, in which case they may be paid out of CAPITAL.

See also ACCUMULATIVE DIVIDEND, CUM-dividend, EX-dividend, FINAL DIVIDEND, INTERIM DIVIDEND, SCRIP DIVIDEND and DIVIDEND RESTRAINT.

The term dividend is also used to refer to the amount of money shared out among the customers of a consumer CO-OPERATIVE SOCIETY.

dividend restraint. As a measure to counter INFLATION a government may urge COMPANIES to reduce the size of DIVIDENDS. This restraint would have the effect of reducing the amount of consumer purchasing power in the economy and thus the *demand-pull*.

division of labour. This is an aspect of SPECIALISATION whereby human economic activity becomes increasingly diversified and specialised. It can be seen as part of the process of economic development and its extent may well be an index of the state of such development in an economy.

The following are the main advantages:
(i) increased output;
(ii) time is saved, in both learning a skill and in passing from one process to another;
(iii) specialisation in a single task increases skill and dexterity;
(iv) there is increased scope for inventiveness when a person concentrates on one job; and
(v) there is economy in the use of equipment as tools and machinery are in use continually and not lying idle while the worker is engaged on another task;
The main disadvantages are as follows:
(i) work may become monotonous and repetition blunt intelligence and artistic taste;

    (ii) physical and nervous strain may be increased if pace is set
       by a machine or other workers;
    (iii) the job may be so narrow in its scope that inventiveness is
       checked; and
    (iv) MOBILITY of labour is checked as specialisation increases,
       and the possibilty of unemployment is greater.
The extent to which the division of labour can proceed is
limited by the extent of the MARKET.

documentary credit. A technique of payment by an importer to
an exporter whereby the former requests his bank to send a letter
to the exporter undertaking to pay him when he receives the
relevant documents drawn up in accordance with the terms already laid down.

double taxation. This occurs when two taxes calculated on the
same tax base are levied and collected in the same period.

double taxation relief. To prevent some incomes from being
taxed twice. For example, if a SHAREHOLDER and the COM-
PANY are in different countries, *double taxation relief* agreements
are made for the remission of tax in one of the countries.

draft. This is a written order relating to a certain sum of money
that a creditor wishes paid by a debtor. It usually involves the
creditor's banker, who will present it to the debtor for his approval, or ACCEPTANCE.

drawback. If a DUTY is imposed on certain imports not destined
for domestic consumption and subsequently exported, the repayment of duty is called a *drawback*.

dumping. The sale of a product in a foreign market at a price
below that at which it is being sold in the domestic market. If it
is possible for two domestic markets to be completely separate,
then domestic *dumping* may take place.

duopoly. A situation in which there are only two producers,
sometimes called a *partial monopoly*.

duosony. A situation in which there are only two buyers of a
product. See BUYER'S MONOPOLY.

duty. TAXATION levied upon the import, export or consumption of home-produced commodities. See CUSTOMS DUTY and
EXCISE DUTY; also AD VALOREM.

econometrics. The application of mathematical and scientific
methods of measurement to economic facts and problems in order
to test and develop theory.

economic. The general usage of this word is a description of
something yielding enough to cover expenses. The economist
applies it to any activity concerned with the creation of an

ECONOMIC GOOD or, more specifically, to the most effective means available for such creation.

economic friction. In economic theory, change can be regarded as being made smoothly; whereas in fact there exist many obstacles of a social and psychological nature to hinder the flexibility and self-adaptability of the ECONOMIC SYSTEM, ie the operation of economic 'forces'. These impediments cause *economic friction*: prejudice, irrational likes and dislikes and customs provide many examples.

economic good. Anything, material or immaterial, that is useful to man, can be obtained, and is in some sense scarce. The term is used for all goods which are not FREE GOODS. See also *capital good* (under CAPITAL), CONSUMER GOOD, GOOD, INFERIOR GOOD, PUBLIC GOOD, UTILITY and WEALTH.

economic growth. This aspect of economics has increasingly attracted the attention of economists since the second world war and can be best defined as taking place when there is an increase in the REAL NATIONAL PRODUCT (see also NATIONAL PRODUCT) of an ECONOMY.

economic history. The study and analysis of economic phenomena from an historical point of view.

economic law. The word 'law' has many meanings, but two are fundamental: a rule, enacted or customary, recognised as binding by a community; or a generalised statement of a particular tendency. An *economic law* is of the latter kind and is a statement of an invariable relationship between specified economic conditions and phenomena.

Economic laws are either very general in their scope, for example, the law of SUPPLY AND DEMAND, and LAW OF DIMINISHING RETURNS, or state, with a degree of probability, that under specified conditions a certain effect will occur.

economic man. The 'economic man' is an abstraction, a hypothetical being whose behaviour is governed solely by economic motives.

economic planning. In general, this refers to any attempt to plan economic activity and anticipate the results. Thus, economic planning is carried on at all levels in the economy although the term is usually used to refer to the governmental direction of economic operations.

Economic Planning Councils. In December 1964, the Secretary of State for Economic Affairs announced proposals for the reorganisation of regional economic planning (see DEVELOPMENT AREAS, etc). The proposals included the setting up of regional councils and boards.

economic rent. See RENT.

economics. Definitions of economics fall loosely into two groups. One is based upon WEALTH and WELFARE and the older definitions fall within its scope. The other group is more recent and is claimed to be more scientific in its approach, which is from the scarcity of resources to their satisfaction of human wants.

Typical of the first group is the definition suggested by Marshall: 'Political Economy or Economics is a study of man's actions in the ordinary business of life: it inquires how he gets his income and how he uses it. . . . Thus it is on the one hand a study of wealth, and on the other, and more important side, a part of the study of man'.

The starting points of the other group of definitions are the recognition of human want and the scarcity of the means to satisfy those wants. The most well-known definition using this approach is that given by Robbins in his *Essay on the Significance of Economic Science*; it is that economics is 'the science which studies human behaviour as a relationship between ends and scarce means which have alternative uses'. That is, it is assumed that resources are inadequate to satisfy all needs, or 'ends', and that choice must be exercised in order that the resources shall be used in the most satisfying way.

This second group stems from the wish to establish the subject as a science both theoretical and positive (ie dealing with matters of fact), and that, as compared with the first group, the type of definition does enable one to decide whether a particular problem is an economic one or not.

economic sanctions. These are economically coercive measures sometimes employed in international affairs in an effort to ensure that decisions collectively made are adhered to.

Economics Association. This was founded in Britain in 1939. Its stated aims include:
 (i) to promote and extend the study of economics and kindred subjects in schools and colleges for examinations and as part of education for citizenship;
 (ii) to provide means for the exchange of views on teaching methods and syllabuses; and
 (iii) to act as a representative body on occasions when the educational interests of economics and kindred subjects are involved.

economic system. The nature of economic life under a particular social system.

economic theory. A body of statements propounding a relationship between economic facts, such facts having been verified by formal investigations of economic activity.

economies of scale. See LARGE-SCALE PRODUCTION.

economist. A person expert in ECONOMICS, or in some branch of the subject.

economy. The word is used in the sense of frugality, but otherwise is largely interchangeable with ECONOMIC SYSTEM.

effective demand. See DEMAND.

elasticity of demand. It is possible that within a certain price range, DEMAND may change proportionately with changes in price, ie there is a constant relationship between the two. Outside that range there may be a more than proportionate, or less than proportionate change in demand than in price. To put it simply, a small change in price may produce a big change in demand; or a big change in price produce little or no change in the amount demanded. In the first case, the demand is said to be *elastic*, and in the second, *inelastic*. We say that demand has an *elasticity*, or an *inelasticity*; one term being a function of the other, so that a high degree of elasticity means a low degree of inelasticity, and vice versa, In general, one can say that the demand for necessities is inelastic and that for luxuries is elastic.

elasticity of supply. The reaction of SUPPLY to a price change will greatly depend upon the nature of the productive process; in particular, the availablity of the FACTORS OF PRODUCTION. A producer may make a rational decision to increase supply because a higher price is obtainable, but be unable to increase production because the FIRM is already working at CAPACITY and additional factors are not readily available. In this case there would be an *inelasticity of supply*. If the productive process is more flexible, then supply will be able to respond to a change in price and supply will be *elastic*. The time element is clearly of considerable significance, as the longer the period of time the more likely it is that supply will respond to price change, particularly when the change is an upward one.

employers' associations. These are groupings of employers existing to further their general interests. Their primary purpose is frequently to enable employers to participate in COLLECTIVE BARGAINING with the TRADE UNIONS, but some of them provide a forum solely for the discussion of questions relating to a particular trade. See CONFEDERATION OF BRITISH INDUSTRY.

employment. In its widest sense, this can mean the use of a FACTOR OF PRODUCTION by a FIRM or governmental institution. More narrowly, the term refers to the engagement of LABOUR. See FULL EMPLOYMENT and UNEMPLOYMENT.

endorsement. A signature usually on the back of some form of NEGOTIABLE INSTRUMENT, by which a third or subsequent party guarantees a payment or establishes transfer of ownership.

end product. A term used to denote that something possessing UTILITY emerges from a productive process.

enterprise. This term is sometimes used interchangeably with FIRM, but is usually used in the sense of the FACTOR OF PRODUCTION which brings together all the other factors and co-ordinates their activities into a productive process, ie 'management'. The function is performed by the ENTREPRENEUR.

entrepôt trade. The trade of a country in the products of other countries; that is, the importing of such products, with the intention of exporting them subsequently.

entrepreneur. The person, or persons, who perform the function of ENTERPRISE; that is, he who makes all the decisions concerning the initiation and conduct of a FIRM. He bears the risks in a business. These are numerous and include all the uncertainties involved in the building up of a new business, the possibility of miscalculating the DEMAND for the product, an unexpected shortage of a vital FACTOR OF PRODUCTION, unexpected competition from another product, the risks involved in a decision to vary the proportions of the factors, and so on.
See NORMAL PROFIT and PROFIT.

equilibrium. See GENERAL EQUILIBRIUM.

equilibrium rate of exchange. An equilibrium EXCHANGE RATE is one that ensures no change in a country's reserves of international means of payments.

equimarginal principle. See MARGINAL RATE OF SUBSTITUTION.

equity. The GOODWILL and residual ASSETS of a COMPANY after allowing for all liabilities.

ergonomics. This is a study concerned with the output of LABOUR and can be defined as a study of posture and dexterity to obtain maximum efficiency with minimum fatigue.

ERNIE. Electronic Random Number Indicating Equipment: used to select winning Premium Savings Bonds (see NATIONAL SAVINGS).

estate duty. See DEATH DUTIES.

Euro-dollar. This is not a special dollar, but is a convenient name applied to US dollars owned by Europeans and held in the USA.

European Atomic Energy Community. This community, better known as Euratom, was set up by the 'Rome Treaties' of 1957, which also established the EUROPEAN ECONOMIC COMMUNITY.
The community was intended to facilitate investment in plant for the peaceful uses of atomic energy; develop research and assure the widest dissemination of technical knowledge. In fact,

by the early 1960s, EAEC had emerged as a mainly non-political research organisation working for the commercial development of atomic power.

European Coal and Steel Community. In April 1951, France, Germany, Italy, Belgium, the Netherlands and Luxembourg signed a draft treaty to establish the ECSC as the first European organisation with a federal type of structure. In the July of 1952 the treaty was ratified by the governments of the six countries; four principal institutions of the community had come into existence by the end of the year. These institutions are:

the High Authority;
the Council of Ministers;
the Common Assembly (or European Parliament); and
the Court of Justice.

The aims of the ECSC were:

(i) to set up a single market in coal and steel;
(ii) to raise living standards through an expanding economy;
(iii) to remove hindrances to the mobility of labour; and
(iv) to take the first step towards the unification of Europe.

By 1955, it had become clear that the establishment of the community had been fully justified by the general economic expansion that had taken place in the member countries. Accordingly, a meeting took place to discuss the widening of the economic unity already achieved. In 1956, draft treaties were drawn up to establish a EUROPEAN ECONOMIC COMMUNITY and a EUROPEAN ATOMIC ENERGY COMMUNITY (or Euratom). These treaties were signed in Rome in 1957 and ratified by the six member governments the same year. The two new communities came into force on 1st January 1958, and the ECSC automatically became an organ of the wider EEC.

European Development Fund. This was established under an annex to the 'Rome Treaty' which set up the EUROPEAN ECONOMIC COMMUNITY.

By the end of 1961, the fund had approved over 220 viable development projects (mostly in the African territories associated with the European Economic Community), and granted some $250 million.

European Economic Community. The successful experiment of the EUROPEAN COAL AND STEEL COMMUNITY strengthened belief in the idea of European unity and in Rome on 25th March 1957, the six countries signed two treaties: one to establish the European Economic Community, with the main features of a COMMON MARKET, and the other to create the EUROPEAN ATOMIC ENERGY COMMUNITY. Both of the treaties provided for applications from other European countries wishing to join the communities, or wishing to enter into some form of association with them.

The EEC treaty proposed a transitional period of between twelve and fifteen years during which customs duties between members must be progressively reduced, and ultimately eliminated; trade restrictions and discriminations (see PROTECTION) and all the other obstacles mentioned above were to be removed; harmonisation of economic and social policies, the common external tariff, and a common agricultural policy established. The treaty provided for three stages in the transitional period, each of which was to take four years, if possible.

The target year of 1970 also applied to the right of a resident of any member country to accept employment, invest capital, move a business, or supply services anywhere else in the community.

The treaty prohibited all trade agreements and concerted practices (see RESTRICTIVE TRADE PRACTICES) which were likely to affect trade between member states and which had as their objective the prevention, restriction or distortion of competition within the EEC.

A limited system of association was provided for in the treaty. Associated countries would benefit from the tariff and quota reductions achieved by full members, while being allowed to maintain against the community certain customs duties levied to protect new industries and raise revenue.

In July 1961, the governments of Britain, Denmark and the Irish Republic made known their intention to seek negotiations with a view to joining the EEC. The negotiations which followed were principally concerned with safeguards for the essential interest of British agriculture and of Commonwealth suppliers to British markets and the need to respect obligations to the other members of the EUROPEAN FREE TRADE ASSOCIATION. During the discussions it was claimed that Britain's entry would transform the character of the EEC, which would then be faced with a multitude of additional problems. In mid-January 1963, the French delegation at the discussions requested that negotiations with Britain should be suspended. After the ministers of the other EEC members had failed to change the French attitude, the negotiations broke down.

In 1967, Britain renewed her efforts to join the EEC.

See EUROPEAN INVESTMENT BANK and EUROPEAN SOCIAL FUND.

European Free Trade Association. In 1958 after the breakdown of negotiations to establish a European Free Trade Area, close contact was maintained between the countries who belonged to the Organisation for European Economic Co-operation and who did not belong to the EEC. They were Austria, Denmark, Norway, Portugal, Sweden, Switzerland and Britain. These countries decided that a union between them could obtain some of the benefits which might have been gained by a FREE TRADE area in Europe and provide a basis from which efforts could be continued to obtain such an area.

In July 1959, a plan for the association was endorsed, and in the following November the 'Stockholm Convention' establishing EFTA was initialled. The association was ratified in May 1960. It binds members to establish a free market in industrial products by the abolition of tariffs and other obstacles to trade over a period of ten years, i.e. by 1970.

In 1961 tariff reductions in EFTA were accelerated to keep abreast with those in the EEC and the dismantling of QUOTA systems began.

After the breakdown of the negotiations between Britain and the EEC at the end of January 1963, a programme of action was prepared to include a speeding up of the time-table for tariff elimination, arrangements for trade in agricultural and fishery products, and co-operation between members on economic and technical matters.

European Fund. See EUROPEAN PAYMENTS UNION.

European Investment Bank. The EIB was set up within the EUROPEAN ECONOMIC COMMUNITY in 1958 to assist investment in the less-developed regions of the community and to help the finance of modernisation and new activities of interest to the EEC.

See also EUROPEAN SOCIAL FUND.

European Monetary Agreement. See EUROPEAN PAYMENTS UNION.

European Payments Union. Before the EPU was created in 1950, there existed in Europe no adequate method by which a country could set off a payments surplus earned in bilateral trade (ie a FAVOURABLE TRADE BALANCE) against a deficit incurred with other countries. The establishment of the EPU provided the vital CLEARING HOUSE through which settlement was possible for transactions between western European countries and between their territories overseas. It was thus an instrument for the liberalisation of international trade.

By the end of 1958, the EPU had become so effective that nearly one-third of the world trade was financed through its machinery.

In the same year the European Monetary Agreement, embodying the European Fund came into operation and the EPU ceased to exist once members whose total quotas represented at least half of the overall total notified that they had restored CONVERTIBILITY. In January 1959, the union was wound up and its residual assets disposed of. Part of these went into the European

Fund, to be used along with contributions from members for the provision of credit facilities.

The EMA instituted a multilateral system of settlements that requires every member to limit currency fluctuations by fixing buying and selling rates for gold, dollars, or any currency. Such rates, ie exchange rates, have to be notified and have to be used for the settlement of indebtedness. Under the revised system, balances notified to the BANK FOR INTERNATIONAL SETTLE-MENTS are not converted at the middle PARITIES, as under the EPU, but at the extreme of the official dealing limits more un-favourable to the country initiating the clearing.

An indirect, but important result of the operations of the EPU and EMA is the co-operation that has been engendered between the CENTRAL BANKS of Europe; for example, see BASLE AGREEMENTS. See also ORGANISATION FOR EUROPEAN CO-OPERATION AND DEVELOPMENT.

European Recovery Programme. This plan, colloquially called the 'Marshall Plan', was one of special aid to Europe to help it to achieve economic rehabilitation. See ORGANISATION FOR ECONOMIC CO-OPERATION AND DEVELOPMENT.

The programme was officially scheduled to finish in 1951, but, in fact, continued after this date in different guises.

European Social Fund. This fund is one of the special agencies established within the EUROPEAN ECONOMIC COMMUNITY. Its purpose is to promote facilities for employment and the MOBI-LITY of workers inside the community.

euro-sterling. The name sometimes given to deposits of sterling held in Europe, eg in the banks of Paris. See EURO-DOLLAR.

ex-. *ex-all:* excluding all the extra advantages attaching to a SECURITY.

ex-cap: shortened form of ex-capitalisation, ie excluding the benefits of a CAPITALISATION ISSUE.

ex-div: abbreviation for *ex-dividend*, ie excluding the right to current DIVIDEND payable on a security.

ex-rights: excluding the right to an issue of securities (see RIGHTS ISSUE).

excess capacity. This means a stock of CAPITAL goods that is owned by a FIRM, but is not in use. See CAPACITY.

exchange. The act of accepting one thing for another, ie BARTER or a transaction involving MONEY. Exchange is a key topic in ECONOMICS, and economists study the mechanism by which a great diversity of exchanges take place in an economy.

An *exchange* is also a place where exchanges take place, eg FOREIGN EXCHANGE market, LONDON COMMODITY EX-CHANGE, STOCK EXCHANGE, etc.

exchange control. This is the control exercised by the state, and usually through the CENTRAL BANK, of all dealings in gold and FOREIGN EXCHANGE. Such control may have its origin in persistently unfavourable BALANCES OF PAYMENTS. The more familiar cause, however, is war, when it is important that the state has access to all available funds for necessary purchases of 'strategic materials' (food, iron ore, etc) from abroad.

See also BLOCKED ACCOUNT, SECURITY STERLING and STERLING BALANCE.

Exchange Equalisation Account. After departing from the GOLD STANDARD in 1931, Britain faced the prospect of wide fluctuations in the exchange value of sterling. As a counter measure a fund was set up which could be used, under the control of the Treasury, for the purchase and sale of gold and foreign currencies in order to prevent such fluctuations.

At the outbreak of war in 1939 and the imposition of far-reaching EXCHANGE CONTROL, the function of the EEA was extended to hold virtually the entire stock of gold then held by the BANK OF ENGLAND. After the war, the purposes for which the fund might be used were extended to include 'the conservation or disposition in the national interest of the means of making payments abroad'. Today, the account is the custodian of the country's reserves of gold and foreign currencies (it operates, in fact, as the reserve not merely for Britain, but for all the SCHEDULED TERRITORIES) and is provided with sterling capital from the CONSOLIDATED FUND SERVICES.

See GOLD AND CONVERTIBLE CURRENCY RESERVE.

exchange rate. Strictly, any PRICE is an exchange rate, but the term is invariably used to refer to the price of one currency in terms of another, ie the proportion in which two different currencies are exchanged.

Exchequer. The central account of the British government kept by the TREASURY at the BANK OF ENGLAND.

See CONSOLIDATED FUND SERVICES and PUBLIC WORKS LOANS BOARD.

Exchequer Bonds. These are short-dated GOVERNMENT SECURITIES, originally with lives of one, two or five years; thus they form part of the *unfunded* or FLOATING DEBT. Once, they were used on a large scale as a means of raising temporary finance for the government, but they are now of far less importance.

excise duty. This is a duty imposed on home-produced goods and domestically provided services. A reason for the imposition of such TAXATION is to offset or limit the protective effects (see PROTECTION) of the imposition of a CUSTOMS DUTY on similar goods imported from abroad. The excise duties levied in Britain on tobacco, alcoholic drink and hydrocarbon oils provide a sizeable proportion of government revenue.

export. An ECONOMIC GOOD sent to another country; also the act of sending it. See IMPORT, INVISIBLES and VISIBLES.

export bounty. A SUBSIDY by a government on specified exports in order to encourage the development of an industry or to increase the country's participation in foreign trade.

Export Credits Guarantee Department. The ECGD is responsible directly to the BOARD OF TRADE and functions to provide insurance for British exporters against the main risks of financial loss incurred in trading with countries. The department is run on commercial lines.
  The risks insurable with the ECGD include the following:
  (i) the insolvency or protracted default of the buyer;
  (ii) government action which blocks or delays payment;
  (iii) war, revolution or other civil disturbance in the buyer's country; or
  (iv) 'any other cause of loss occurring outside the United Kingdom and not within the control of the exporter or buyer, and not normally insurable with commercial insurers'.
See also INSURANCE EXPORT FINANCE COMPANY.

external account. See NON-RESIDENT ACCOUNT.

extractive industry. This term is used either for an INDUSTRY taking materials directly from LAND or one which produces or uses extracts, such as dyes and tannin.

face value. The NOMINAL VALUE printed or written on a document, bank note, coin, etc. The MARKET VALUATION may be higher or lower.

factor. An agent or deputy; in commerce, a representative who buys and sells goods on behalf of his principal. He does this on a commission basis, and his commission is called *factorage*. See FACTORS OF PRODUCTION.

factor cost. This refers to the amount in the MARKET PRICE of a product due to the FACTORS OF PRODUCTION employed to produce it. The main item in the *market price* thus excluded is usually an *indirect tax* (see TAXATION).

factors of production. PRODUCTION clearly results from the interaction of various agencies and the economist attempts to classify them. The traditional classification is into the following groups of factors or *agents of production*: LAND, LABOUR, CAPITAL and ENTERPRISE.

FAS. Free alongside. See CIF, FOB and FOR.

favourable trade balance. The BALANCE OF TRADE is 'favourable' or 'active' when the value of VISIBLE exports exceeds that of visible imports in a given period of time. See UNFAVOURABLE TRADE BALANCE.

fiat money. *Paper money* that is inconvertible (see CONVERTIBILITY) and unsupported by specie or reserves. See MONEY.

fiduciary issue. A fiduciary issue of money is one that is not backed by gold or silver. In Britain the entire issue of BANK OF ENGLAND notes (now over £3,000 million) is of this nature and backed only by GOVERNMENT SECURITIES. The first British fiduciary issue was provided for in 1844 by the BANK CHARTER ACT, when the total was fixed at £14 million.
See FIAT MONEY and MONEY.

final dividend. The last distribution of profits to be made in respect of a trading period (usually a year). Earlier distributions are INTERIM DIVIDENDS. See also DIVIDEND.

finance company. This is a rather vague name that is sometimes applied to firms engaged in HIRE PURCHASE finance.

Finance Corporation for Industry. This is an investment institution which was founded in 1945 to provide finance for companies unable to obtain it through normal channels. It is particularly concerned with the provision of temporary funds for industrial development unable to attract capital until nearer its earning stage. Once funds are obtainable from normal sources, it is intended that the FCI loan be replaced.
The minimum facility given is £200,000. This is because the INDUSTRIAL AND COMMERCIAL FINANCE CORPORATION LTD was established at the same time as the FCI to make available sums up to this amount.

finance house. Consumers can obtain credit in various ways, but the most common is through HIRE PURCHASE. When this method is used the retailer may finance the transaction himself, or he may lodge his hire purchase agreements with a *finance house* and obtain an advance against them. The customer pays instalments to the retailer, who acts as an agent for the finance house and pays off the advance at a rate based on the instalments due to him. See INDUSTRIAL BANK.

firm. The production unit, whether it comprises a one-man firm or a large-scale undertaking with thousands of shareholders and employees. A number of firms producing similar goods or services make up an INDUSTRY; if the firm makes up the industry a MONOPOLY exists.

fiscal. Concerned with MONEY and CREDIT, particularly PUBLIC FINANCE.

fiscal policy. Fundamentally, this is the policy pursued by a government for raising the revenue necessary to meet its expenditure. It embraces the scope and degree of TAXATION, NATIONAL DEBT, government borrowing, etc. An important aspect of any fiscal policy today is the intended effect of its legislation and administration practices upon the private and public sectors of the economy.

fixed charge. A charge on specific ASSETS made to secure a debt; often the subject of a DEBENTURE. See FLOATING CHARGE.

fixed trust. A type of TRUST (see INVESTMENT TRUST and UNIT TRUST) investing in a fixed portfolio of SECURITIES. The shareholders own units of CAPITAL, which represent a portion of the trust's investment. The portfolio, or list, is established by the 'trust deed', and a definite number and proportion of the underlying securities forms a unit.

flexible trust. A UNIT TRUST in which the portfolio of SECURITIES can be varied; sometimes called a *managed trust*.

flight from currency. An expression sometimes used to describe what is happening when foreign holders of a country's currency sell it in anticipation of a fall in its value.

floating charge. A floating charge is one made by the holder of a DEBENTURE upon a company's stock or its book debts. See FIXED CHARGE.

floating debt. Any debt that is short-term by nature; but in particular this term refers to that part of NATIONAL DEBT that is not long-term (see FUNDED DEBT). It is sometimes called *unfunded debt*.

floating exchange. An EXCHANGE RATE with no fixed PARITY so that the exchange can freely float at the level determined by supply and demand.

flotation. The starting of an enterprise, usually a COMPANY. Thus, the term is sometimes applied to the raising of new CAPITAL by subscription.

FOB. Free on board. A term referring to the payment for goods when the price does not include charges for insurance and shipment. Compare with CIF and see also FAS and FOR.

FOR. Free on rail. See CIF, FAS and FOB.

foreign bill. A COMMERCIAL BILL that has been drawn in one country and is payable in another. See also INLAND BILL.

foreign exchange. This is concerned with the exchange of one foreign currency for another. The demand for a foreign currency arises out of indebtedness incurred in INTERNATIONAL TRADE;

investment in another country; tourism and business travel; speculation concerning changes in EXCHANGE RATES; and various governmental needs.

See also EXCHANGE CONTROL.

forward exchange. This is a type of FOREIGN EXCHANGE transaction whereby a contract is made to exchange one currency for another at a fixed date in the future at a specified EXCHANGE RATE.

frame. See SAMPLING FRAME.

free good. Free goods are those external to man, inherently useful and in such plentiful supply that as much can be had as is desired without conscious effort. Fresh air and sunshine would normally be examples of free goods.

See GOOD, capital good (under CAPITAL), CONSUMER GOOD, LAND, PUBLIC GOOD, UTILITY and WEALTH.

free list. A list of commodities on which no CUSTOMS DUTY is levied.

free market. A MARKET in which buyers and sellers are free to trade, ie in which no compulsion is exercised and no restrictions exist concerning prices and amounts.

free trade. This refers to INTERNATIONAL TRADE unhindered by any kind of PROTECTION.

See GENERAL AGREEMENT ON TARIFFS AND TRADE.

frequency chart. See DISTRIBUTION.

frequency distribution. See DISTRIBUTION.

frequency table. See DISTRIBUTION.

fringe benefit. A reward received by an employee in addition to the monetary wages paid for actual work done.

frozen. This term is used in contradistinction to LIQUID and suggests that conversion into money is difficult or impossible. 'Frozen' ASSETS or CAPITAL are 'illiquid' and would be difficult or impossible to sell and, if convertible, probably at considerable loss.

full employment. According to Lord Beveridge, this means 'having always more vacant jobs than unemployed men'. It does not mean a complete absence of UNEMPLOYMENT for this would be impossible in a dynamic economy, but it does mean a maximum of, say, 3 per cent of the WORKING POPULATION unemployed. On the other hand, should the level of unemployment fall markedly below this, then a situation of *over-full employment* may exist with the demand for labour too high and the pressure of INFLATION evident. *Over-full employment* has often been a problem in Britain since the second world war.

fundamental disequilibrium. This term is used in the Articles of the INTERNATIONAL MONETARY FUND to imply a persistent substantial discrepancy between the PURCHASING POWER PARITY and the PAR EXCHANGE RATE of a nation's currency.

funded debt. In Britain, this refers to the part of the NATIONAL DEBT that is long-term. Originally, it was that part of the debt the interest on which was secured by a specific fund. Now, it is the more or less permanent part represented by CONSOLS, Consolidated Loan, War Loan, etc, ie that part of the national debt that is not unfunded (see FLOATING DEBT).

funding. The process whereby short-term (or FLOATING) debt is converted into long-term (or FUNDED) debt.

Gaussian Curve. See NORMAL CURVE.

gearing. This is obtained by dividing the amount of 'fixed interest capital' (including PRIOR CHARGES) into the 'ordinary capital' (see CAPITAL and SECURITIES). If there is a high proportion of the former to the latter, then the company is said to be 'highly geared' and a small change in profits can make a considerable difference to the amount available for distribution to the owners of the EQUITY.

General Agreement on Tariffs and Trade. In Geneva, in 1947, a Trade Conference was held at which 23 nations were represented. During the conference a multilateral agreement called the General Agreement on Tariffs and Trade was signed.

The preamble to the agreement says that the contracting parties should enter 'into reciprocal and mutually advantageous arrangements directed to the substantial reduction of tariffs and other barriers to trade and to the elimination of discriminatory treatment in international commerce'. In Part I of the agreement each signatory was required to give all other signatories any 'advantage, favour, privilege or immunity' that it had already accorded to any one 'most-favoured-nation'. In Part II of the agreement there are provisions intended to make sure that the advantages from tariff reductions cannot be reduced in other ways, for instance, through changes in quantitative import controls. Part III of the agreement deals mainly with problems of enforcement.

GATT operates by holding periodic conferences, and since the initial one in Geneva it has met in Annecy and Torquay.

In addition to its work in the field of tariffs and quantitative restriction, GATT also does valuable service in connection with export subsidies, customs, formalities taxation, etc.

See also CUSTOMS DUTY, DISCRIMINATORY DUTY, FREE TRADE, IMPORT QUOTAS, MOST-FAVOURED-NATION CLAUSES and TARIFFS.

general equilibrium. This is a concept used in ECONOMIC THEORY to describe a state of affairs in which there is no tendency for things to change as a result of the operation of economic forces.

general union. See TRADE UNION.

geometric mean. This may be defined as the antilogarithm of the sum of the logarithms of the values in a group divided by the number of values. That is, it is the nth root of the product of n items. See CENTRAL TENDENCY.

Giffen good. See INFERIOR GOOD.

gilt-edged securities. These are SECURITIES carrying the least amount of risk, and are usually issued by governments. See GOVERNMENT SECURITIES.

giro. The giro system is a system of CREDIT TRANSFER. It means that a single direct instruction is given to credit money to a designated account. The giro is used by most European countries and is more comprehensive than the *bank credit transfer scheme* introduced in Britain in 1961. The system is in almost all cases operated by the Post Office. In 1965, it was announced that a giro was to be established in Britain.

give-on. See CONTANGO.

Gold and Convertible Currency Reserve. One of the functions of the BANK OF ENGLAND is to act as banker for the Sterling Area (see SCHEDULED TERRITORIES), and this fact plus the extensive world trade of Britain and the wide use of sterling for the settlement of international accounts, poses a big problem for the monetary authorities. This is the need to maintain a balance between payments and receipts for foreign transactions. A deficit as a result of trade must be met either by obtaining credit, or by immediate settlement, which means drawing upon whatever reserves of gold or foreign currencies are possessed. If such reserves were very large then fluctuations in the British BALANCE OF PAYMENTS would never present an immediate problem; but the reserves, in fact, have long been very low. The essential attribute of the Scheduled Territories system is that the reserves of Britain also contain the reserves of the whole area, and that the function of the reserves is to bridge the gap between the debits arising out of the trade between the area and the rest of the world.

At the outbreak of the second world war the EXCHANGE EQUALISATION ACCOUNT became the repository of the gold and dollar reserve of the area. It was called the 'gold and dollar reserve' as there was a great scarcity of dollars and it was decided that London should become the guardian of dollars earned by the countries in the Sterling Area. The scarcity of dollars con-

tinued well into the 1950s and it was not until the advent of
CONVERTIBILITY at the end of 1958 that the accent upon dollars
was removed.

The reserve is now known as the Gold and Convertible Currency Reserve.

gold standard. Gold standard means the measurement of values
in terms of gold; it is the name given to the international monetary system that predominated before 1914. A country is said to
be on the gold standard proper when its monetary unit is defined
in terms of gold of a certain weight and fineness; gold coins are
LEGAL TENDER and circulate freely; the authorities are willing
to accept BULLION and convert it into coins; when gold can be
freely bought and sold, exported and imported; and when the
value of other forms of money are maintained at a par with the
gold coins.

The *gold specie*, or *currency standard*, was finally suspended in
Britain in 1914, having lasted in this 'classic' form for some 98
years. In April 1925, Britain and many other countries restored
it in a modified form, called the *gold bullion standard*, which
lasted until September 1931, when it was irrevocably suspended.

good. Anything, material or immaterial, exterior to man and
useful to him. The term does not imply an ethical or legal meaning, in fact, a commodity harmful to man but desired by him is a
good to the economist. See *capital good* (under CAPITAL), CONSUMER GOOD, ECONOMIC GOOD, FREE GOOD, INFERIOR
GOOD, PUBLIC GOOD, UTILITY and WEALTH.

goodness of fit. A test for this makes a comparison of the
expected frequencies (from a THEORETICAL DISTRIBUTION)
with observed frequencies to decide whether or not the differences
involved can be attributed to chance.

goodwill. When a business changes hands, continuity of prosperity is likely to be assured if the previous owner, or owners, have
built up a good reputation. The probability of such continuity is
regarded as an ASSET of an 'intangible' nature, and an assessment of its value will be recorded in a 'goodwill account'. See
also *fixed capital* under CAPITAL.

government broker. The BANK OF ENGLAND does not enter
the STOCK EXCHANGE to buy and sell GOVERNMENT SECURITIES; all operations in the GILT-EDGED market are conducted
through a firm of STOCKBROKERS, whose representative is
called the *Government Broker*. It is to him that instructions are
given by the government through the Bank to buy or sell government securities.

See also OPEN MARKET OPERATIONS and FUNDED DEBT.

government debt. See NATIONAL DEBT.

government securities. The expressions *gilt-edged* or *government bonds, securities* or *stocks* are all taken in the RADCLIFFE REPORT (para 16c) 'to refer to the securities issued by Her Majesty's Government (or by nationalised industries and guaranteed by Her Majesty's Government) that are dealt in on the London Stock Exchange; these terms do not include Treasury Bills'.

See also CONSOLS, FUNDED DEBT, NATIONAL DEBT and TREASURY BILL.

grading. In the *commodity markets* (see LONDON COMMODITY EXCHANGE) the establishment of 'grades' according to the quality of the commodity is of considerable assistance in transactions. A transaction can take place without inspection, even of a sample, if a recognised grade is concerned.

gross. A total without deductions, not NET.

gross dividend. This term is usually used to describe a DIVIDEND before it has been taxed.

gross income. An INCOME before any deduction has been made, eg for a FIRM it would represent total receipts before the subtraction of the COSTS or *expenses of production*; for an individual, his income before the deduction of INCOME TAX (and see TAX).

gross profit. Has been defined as TURNOVER less the total of the purchase prices of the goods sold in a retail business. See MARK-UP and PROFIT.

ground rent. Rent, in the commercial sense, that is paid to a landlord for the use of land without improvements. The payment of ground rent gives the lessee the right to improve the land (eg build on it) and occupy it. See RENT.

group banking. See CHAIN BANKING.

guaranteed price. See SUPPORT.

hammered, hammering. An announcement made by the Council of the STOCK EXCHANGE when a member cannot meet his obligations.

hard currency. In general, a currency that is scarce. The most likely circumstances in which the demand for a currency exceeds the supply of it are those when there is a high demand for the exports of the country concerned. In other words, when some or all other countries have an *unfavourable* BALANCE OF PAYMENTS on current account with the country whose currency is 'hard'. See SOFT CURRENCY.

harmonic mean. This is the reciprocal of the ARITHMETIC MEAN of the reciprocals of all the values. See CENTRAL TENDENCY.

hedging. To hedge is to protect oneself against loss should events take an unforeseen course.

hire purchase. A hire purchase agreement is a hiring of goods coupled with an option to purchase. The hirer is *not* a person who has brought or agreed to buy goods and, therefore, he cannot pass good title to a third party. When goods are selected by a consumer who wishes to use hire purchase, the dealer immediately sells the goods to a FINANCE HOUSE, INDUSTRIAL BANK, etc, with which the hirer (ie the consumer) enters into a CONTRACT of hire purchase. Under the agreement, the hirer undertakes to pay to the owner instalments as specified in the contract. The consumer is not the buyer until he has paid all instalments and then exercises his 'option to purchase'. The dealer may have sufficient resources to finance the hire purchase himself.

A *credit sale* differs from a hire purchase agreement in that the parties are buyer and seller, who have entered into agreement (for the sale of goods) under which payment is to be made at a specified time or times after the contract of sale (ie the buyer normally gets possession of the goods before he has paid for them). A credit sale is sometimes known as *instalment buying*.

hoarding. The accumulation of goods not intended for immediate consumption. In the case of money, this is hoarded when it is accumulated and put to no use at all, viz it goes out of circulation and the effective supply of money is reduced. See QUANTITY THEORY OF MONEY and SAVING.

holding company. A COMPANY owning a sufficient amount of the SECURITIES of another company to control it. This type of firm can hide its real size and occupy the apex of a huge pyramid of other companies. In Britain, Imperial Chemical Industries and Vickers are good examples.

horizontal expansion. The growth of a firm by the absorption or construction of extra facilities to meet an increase in the firm's productive activities. See INTEGRATION.

horizontal trade union. See CRAFT UNION and TRADE UNION.

hot money. This term usually refers to short-term movements of *money-capital* (see CAPITAL) between countries.

illiquid. See LIQUID.

immobility. See MOBILITY.

impact of a tax. This is where a tax is first paid. The burden of it may fall elsewhere and, in fact, may be shifted again and again. See INCIDENCE OF TAXATION and TAXATION.

imperfect competition. A state of COMPETITION in which there is imperfection because of influential positions held by buyers or sellers or both. Thus, in a MARKET situation wherein prices can be abnormally influenced, PERFECT COMPETITION cannot exist. This may be called *monopolistic competition*.

See also DUOPOLY, DUOSONY, MONOPOLY and OLIGOPOLY, and PRODUCT DIFFERENTIATION.

import. As a noun: an ECONOMIC GOOD received from another country. As a verb: to receive such goods. See EXPORT, INVISIBLES and VISIBLES.

import duty. See DUTY.

import quota. A definite maximum quantity of a commodity that may be imported within a specified period of time.

import surcharge. In October 1964, the severe deficit in Britain's BALANCE OF PAYMENTS led the government to break a number of international agreements by imposing an import surcharge of 15 per cent on all imports, with the exception of foodstuffs, basic industrial raw materials, etc. In April 1965 the rate was reduced to 10 per cent and it was removed altogether the following November.

incentive. This is loosely used to describe a device intended to urge labour to greater productive efforts.

incidence of taxation. Where the ultimate burden of a tax falls notwithstanding the manner in which it is levied. The 'incidence' is on the consumer, but the IMPACT OF A TAX is on the seller, or one of the sellers, involved.

income. The monetary or non-monetary return to a FACTOR OF PRODUCTION as reward for productive activity. See INTEREST, KEYNESIAN ECONOMICS, PROFIT, RENT and WAGES.

incomes policy. See WAGES POLICY.

income tax. This is usually taken to mean a tax on the INCOMES of individuals. In Britain, the tax dates from 1797, when it was introduced as a special measure to help finance the war effort. It was originally only a temporary measure and was, in fact, repealed in 1816. However, this type of tax was re-imposed in 1842 and has been in existence since then. It is now a vital part of Britain's FISCAL system.

The term often embraces the incomes of COMPANIES (see PROFIT), in which guise it may be called a *companies tax*. See TAXATION.

inconvertible note issue. See CONVERTIBILITY.

increasing returns. DIMINISHING PRODUCTIVITY or *returns* postulates that when increments of a variable FACTOR OF PRODUCTION are increasingly combined with a fixed factor, a point will be arrived at after which the additions to output will diminish. It may be assumed, therefore, that up to a certain point the additions to total output will, in some cases, be increasing. Increasing returns may also result from the re-arrangement of a fixed supply of factors, or if the productivity of one or more is increased, eg by DIVISION OF LABOUR.

See also MARGIN, etc.

index bonds. These are BONDS on which the money value of the DIVIDENDS, and of the capital payment at MATURITY, would not be fixed at the time of issue but would vary according to some index (see INDEX NUMBER) of the purchasing power of money.

index number. A device used to show relative changes in economic phenomena over a period of time. The usual practice is to choose a 'base year' and assign to it the value 100. It is then possible to show subsequent percentage changes in prices, costs, production, etc.

Examples of index numbers in use:

Prices—'Index of Retail Prices' compiled by the Ministry of Labour. It measures the change from month to month in the average level of prices of the commodities and services purchased by the great majority of households in Britain, including practically all wage-earners and most small and medium salary earners.

'Index of Wholesale Prices' compiled by the magazine *Statist* (publication ceased in 1967): the base period for this index goes back to the Sauerbeck index, thus providing comparisons with 1846. The Board of Trade and the magazine *The Economist* also compile wholesale price indices.

See SHARE INDEX.

indifference curve. An *indifference curve* is used to show diagrammatically a range of combinations of two commodities or services (measured one along each axis of a graph) each of which combination yields the same satisfaction, or total UTILITY, as the others.

See also MARGINAL RATE OF SUBSTITUTION and OPPORTUNITY CURVE.

indirect production. See ROUNDABOUT PRODUCTION.

indirect taxation. See TAXATION.

induced consumption. When CAPITAL FORMATION has the effect of increasing CONSUMPTION, this is said to be 'induced'. The increase in consumption derives first from the capital goods industries as more labour is employed and as rewards increase. Secondly, as labour in the consumer goods industries benefits, so it makes its contribution to increase further consumption. See ACCELERATOR and *multiplier* (under KEYNESIAN ECONOMICS).

Industrial and Commercial Finance Corporation. The ICFC was established in 1945 by the BANK OF ENGLAND, the London CLEARING BANKS and the Scottish banks. It provides long-term (10 to 20 years) credit for industrial businesses in Britain, particularly where the existing facilities provided by the banks and STOCK EXCHANGE are not easily available.

It was felt that credit below £5,000 could be met by the banks and this figure constitutes the minimum limit of the ICFC facilities. It was also considered that above £200,000, capital requirements could be catered for by the NEW ISSUE MARKET, the FINANCE CORPORATION FOR INDUSTRY and other credit institutions.

industrial bank. A financial institution making relatively small loans to individuals on terms which provide for regular (weekly or monthly) instalment payments. In other words, an industrial bank provides CREDIT by HIRE PURCHASE, ie medium-term credit.

See also FINANCE HOUSE.

Industrial Court. The Industrial Court was established under the Industrial Courts Act of 1919 which gave effect to the recommendations made in a report of the WHITLEY COMMITTEE.

The court is a permanent and independent tribunal; it is not a court of law and its decisions are not legally enforceable, but once a decision has been accepted or acted upon it forms a condition of the contract of employment.

See also COLLECTIVE BARGAINING, JOINT INDUSTRIAL COUNCILS, etc.

industrial inertia. The tendency of an industry or industries to remain located in an area after the advantages of location in that area are no longer significant. See LOCATION OF INDUSTRY.

industrial relations. The relationships between workers and their employers. See ARBITRATION, CONCILIATION, INDUSTRIAL COURT, JOINT INDUSTRIAL COUNCILS, WAGES COUNCILS, etc.

Industrial Reorganisation Corporation. The IRC was set up in January 1966 to begin to meet the long recognised need for more RATIONALISATION and concentration in British industry [to promote efficiency and improve our competitiveness in export markets, that is, 'to promote rationalisation schemes which could yield substantial benefits to the national economy'].

industrial training board. Under the Industrial Training Act of 1964, the government began the setting up of *industrial training boards*. The purpose of these is to improve the quality of training and to spread the cost of such training more fairly between one employer and another.

industrial union. A TRADE UNION to which membership is admitted for all workers, skilled or unskilled, in a particular industry.

See CRAFT UNION.

industry. This term is almost exclusively used in a collective sense: a group of FIRMS producing identical or similar products or products having raw materials or uses in common; or more widely to all productive activity in a given area, eg British industry. Often 'industry' is used in a sense that precludes COMMERCE, but, strictly, 'trading' is productive activity and it is possible to refer to, say, the RETAIL industry.

inelastic demand. See ELASTICITY OF DEMAND.

inelastic supply. See ELASTICITY OF SUPPLY.

inertia. Any tendency for economic phenomena to remain as they are (see INDUSTRIAL INERTIA and MOBILITY).

infant industry. A newly established INDUSTRY, or one long established but in a relatively undeveloped state. It has often been argued that such industries are particularly vulnerable to competition from the products of well-established industries in other countries and that the 'infant industries' should be protected (see PROTECTION) by import duties.
See DUTY, COMPARATIVE ADVANTAGES, FREE TRADE, GENERAL AGREEMENT ON TARIFFS AND TRADE.

inference. The process whereby properties of a POPULATION are estimated from the analysis of a SAMPLE.

inferior good. It has been observed that the DEMAND for certain GOODS may increase with a rise in the price of those goods. This paradoxical reaction is said to apply in the case of 'inferior' or *Giffen goods*. For example, if, in the case of a very poor family, expenditure on cheap foodstuffs takes a high proportion of the household income, then a rise in the price of these commodities might result in a decision to spend even less of the income on 'luxuries' and buy more of the cheap foods.

inflation. Basically a situation in which prices are rising and pressures exist to accentuate the fall in the value of money. If, for example, incomes increase and this increase in the volume of money available for exchange transactions is not required by or followed by an appropriate expansion in the number of transactions then a situation exists in which prices will tend to rise. Should income spending fall (or hoarding increase) and the number of exchange transactions fall even more, then a similar tendency exists.
An increase in income spending is sometimes called the 'demand-pull'; it may arise if the quantity of money in circulation is expanded. A similar effect would result if money circulated more quickly as a result of more purchases, ie an increase in the *velocity of circulation* (see QUANTITY THEORY OF MONEY).
This may be called 'demand inflation' for, as effective demand

increases (whether because of higher wages—the 'wage-pull'—easier financial conditions or other reasons), output and employment are pushed up. If the CAPACITY of the economy is under-utilised and there is UNEMPLOYMENT, there is no problem. But, if the general increase in activity means an increase in the demand for a limited supply of the factors, eg raw materials, then shortages develop, labour difficulties tend to arise, a 'cost-push' develops and the prices of products rise.

It is accepted that the monetary authorities are duty bound to attempt to control an inflation should it threaten the stability of the currency, either internally or externally. There are serious inconveniences in using money that fluctuates in value; if a reasonable measure of stability is not preserved the whole basis on which economic activity rests is threatened. Expenditure and income are measured in monetary units and with unstable units the planning of future activity becomes difficult and adds to existing uncertainties.

inflationary gap. The excess of income spending over that required to keep the FACTORS OF PRODUCTION fully employed. In other words, a situation in which the pressure of demand tends to raise the price level. See DEFLATION, DEFLATIONARY GAP and INFLATION.

infra-structure. An economy's CAPITAL in the form of roads, railways, water supplies, educational facilities, health services, etc, without which INVESTMENT in factories, machinery, tools, etc, cannot be fully productive. Its characteristics are that it is often SELF-LIQUIDATING and has a high CAPITAL-OUTPUT RATIO. The absence of *infra-structure* restrains the rate of ECONOMIC GROWTH of under-developed countries.

inheritance tax. See DEATH DUTIES.

inland bill. A COMMERCIAL BILL drawn and payable in one country only. In some ways it is similar to a PROMISSORY NOTE and although quite common in Britain in the first half of the nineteenth century, by the last quarter they had been largely displaced by the CHEQUE.

input. See RAW MATERIAL.

input-output analysis. This is an analysis of the production of different industries illustrating the interrelationships between them and, perhaps, the government and consumers. These relationships are what industries buy from each other and supply to the consumer. Thus, the analysis shows the income of the industries, where it came from, and where it went. This makes it easier to trace the known or possible effects of some external change, eg in the supply of a raw material, its price, or in a change in an industry's markets.

inscribed stock. SECURITIES for which no actual certificates are granted to holders, but whose names and the amount of stock they hold are inscribed in a register kept for the purpose at the banks having the management of the stocks.

instalment credit. See HIRE PURCHASE.

institutional economics. Economics expressed in a way that lays stress upon the influence of social institutions upon economic behaviour.

institutional investor. An institution that invests, as opposed to an individual who invests. Banks, insurance companies and trusts are *institutional investors* and the term might be applied to those companies investing to administer pension schemes.

insurance. An arrangement whereby one party (the insurer) agrees in return for a *premium* to provide *indemnity* for another party (the insured) in the event of some specified loss. Insurance is protection against such risks as accidents, fire, crop failure, the advent of twins, ill health, etc.

Insurance Export Finance Company. In 1962, with the encouragement of the Bank of England, about sixty British insurance institutions combined to establish the IEFC with the purpose of providing longer-term finances for export credit than normally fell within the scope of BANK CREDIT.

intangible asset. See ASSET.

integration. When two or more FIRMS unite in some form or other the process is variously called 'absorption', AMALGAMATION, fusion, MERGER or TAKE-OVER, and sometimes *integration*. Horizontal integration is the production of many different sorts of articles at the same stage of production.

Where a firm performs consecutive processes, ie different stages of production and/or distribution, it is vertically integrated.

Diagonal integration means the provision of auxiliary goods or services required for the several main processes. For instance, a firm may make its own machines, tools, power, etc and thus help a number of lines or successive processes. Integration can, therefore, clearly be backward towards the raw materials, or forward towards the market.

Integration can generally be assumed to yield certain economies, but it is not always a sign of efficiency.

See also CARTEL, HOLDING COMPANY, LARGE-SCALE PRODUCTION and TRUST.

interest. A sum, usually expressed as a 'rate' or percentage, paid for the use of CAPITAL.

The classical view of interest is that it is a reward for saving, a payment for the risk and trouble involved in making a loan, a cost of investment and that the rate is determined by the inter-action of the demand for loans and the supply of loanable funds.

This view is too simple, particularly on the supply side, and later views, notably those of Keynes, have stressed the LIQUID-ITY aspect. Long before Keynes, interest had been described as a payment made to a lender because the borrower prefers funds now to the future and the satisfaction of immediate wants holds a higher place on the borrower's scale of preference than on the lender's. Thus, the lender gives up immediate enjoyment of his funds. The 'Monetary Theory' of KEYNESIAN ECONOMICS deals more carefully with this last point under the heading of LIQUIDITY PREFERENCE, that is, the preference that people have to keep their resources as cash or as near to cash as possible. In other words, the need for money for the motives of transac-tions, caution and speculation represents demand, and, in Britain, the Treasury, acting through the Bank of England and commercial banks, determines supply.

See also COMPOUND and SIMPLE INTEREST and SAVING.

interim dividend. The distribution of profits made on account of those earned in a trading period, ie before the FINAL DIVIDEND.

interlocking directorate. This occurs when the director of one COMPANY is also the director of another.

International Bank for Reconstruction and Development. One result of the financial conference at Bretton Woods, USA, in July 1944 was the establishment of this bank. It began operations in 1945 with the initial purpose of assisting economies to re-cover from the consequences of war by the provision of capital. The long-term aim of the 'world bank' is to help the economic development of all member countries either by lending to governmental agencies or private enterprise when no other source of capital is available, or by guaranteeing private loans.

In 1956, the IBRD established the International Finance Corporation; in 1960 the International Development Associa-tion and, late in 1961, the Development Advisory Service, to provide resident experts to help the development programmes of under-developed countries.

international economics. That part of ECONOMICS dealing with the international aspects of trade, finance, specialisation, etc.

International Labour Organisation. The ILO was established in 1919 to promote social justice by the raising of living and working standards and by increasing social security all over the world. In May 1946, it became affiliated to the United Nations as a *specialised agency* and has since been engaged in the provision of technical assistance for various development programmes.

international liquidity. This refers to current financial assets which are widely acceptable for the settlement of international indebtedness.

International Monetary Fund. One of the results of the Bretton Woods financial conference in 1944 was the establishment of the IMF two years later. The fund was designed to promote stability in the foreign exchanges (see PAR EXCHANGE RATE), to maintain orderly exchange arrangements among its members and, in general, to assist in the establishment of a multilateral system of payments in respect of current transactions between members.

The prime function of the fund can now be seen to be the provision of short-term financial aid for member countries in BALANCE OF PAYMENTS difficulties. It usually does this by providing members with foreign currencies in which they are in short supply in exchange for deposits of the members' currencies.

The financial resources of the IMF are supplied by the members, who number over 100. Each has a quota and, normally, 25 per cent of it is paid to the fund in gold and the remainder in the member's own currency.

In addition, the IMF advises on financial policy and helps to train governmental and central bank staffs.

international trade. The trade carried on between different countries. See COMPARATIVE ADVANTAGES, FREE TRADE, GENERAL AGREEMENT ON TARIFFS AND TRADE, etc.

interquartile range. This is the range of values between the lower and upper QUARTILES. See SEMI-INTERQUARTILE RANGE.

introduction. The offer of a NEW ISSUE to the public not directly but through the STOCK EXCHANGE. See also ISSUING HOUSE, OFFER FOR SALE and PLACING.

investment. Investment is the conversion of monetary resources into illiquid (see LIQUID) resources, ie WEALTH. Or, put another way, the use of *money capital* for the acquisition of *capital goods* (see CAPITAL).

See INTEREST, KEYNESIAN ECONOMICS, PROFITS, SAVINGS, etc.

investment trust. Investment trusts are COMPANIES which use their resources to buy SECURITIES of various kinds with the object of distributing the income therefrom to their shareholders. They are thus able to offer the small 'investor' the minimum of risk by diversity of security and accumulated expertise.

See also FIXED TRUST, FLEXIBLE TRUST and UNIT TRUST.

invisibles: exports and imports. The term 'invisibles' is used for all those current transactions featuring in the BALANCE OF PAYMENTS not representing trade in goods. They can be divided into four main groups:

(i) the value of services provided to or received from other countries;

(ii) income received on all forms of investment abroad;

(iii) current payments and receipts by governments; and

(iv) gifts and similar transactions not included under (iii).

See VISIBLES.

irredeemable. See REDEEMABLE.

issue. An *issue* is a block of SECURITIES being sold by a company. The term is also applied to the OFFER FOR SALE and allotment of the securities to the public. See also INTRODUCTION, ISSUE FOR CASH, ISSUING HOUSE, NEW ISSUE and PLACING.

issue for cash. An ISSUE for which a cash payment is required as opposed to a CAPITALISATION ISSUE or an issue in consideration for the purchase of another undertaking.

issuing house. An issuing house acts as an agent between those seeking long-term capital and those willing to provide it. As the RADCLIFFE REPORT puts it: 'the issuing houses make themselves responsible to their clients for the funds they require. . . . Their function is essentially to act as sponsors and underwriters rather than as a source of finance; but the fact that an issuing house stands behind an issue makes it easier to raise the money, and allows a borrower to proceed with his plans, perhaps in advance of the issue, without fear that he may not after all get the full amount he needs.'

See UNDERWRITER.

jobber. This term sometimes refers to a merchant middleman who buys from a manufacturer or importer and sells to wholesalers or retailers. But, its more familiar meaning in Britain is a dealer in SECURITIES on a STOCK EXCHANGE who buys and sells from and to other members of the exchange.

joint demand. The DEMAND which exists when two or more ECONOMIC GOODS must be used together, ie joint demand is the composite of the demands for goods which are used at, or nearly at, the same time. For example, the building of a house means a joint demand for bricks, sand, cement, timber, glass, etc. See also ALTERNATE DEMAND, COMPOSITE DEMAND, DEFERRED DEMAND, DERIVED DEMAND, etc.

Joint Industrial Council. The WHITLEY COMMITTEE ON RELATIONS BETWEEN EMPLOYERS AND EMPLOYED of 1916 recommended amongst other things 'the establishment for each

industry of an organisation, representative of employers and
workpeople, to have as its object the regular consideration of
matters affecting the progress and well-being of the trade from
the point of view of all those engaged in it, so far as this is consistent with the general interests of the community'.

The British government was urged thereby to propose to
employees' and employers' organisations the formation of
Joint Industrial Councils.

By 1938 there were forty-five. The second world war gave an
impetus to the establishment of voluntary negotiating machinery,
as did post-war conditions, and by the 1960s about 200 of the
councils were in existence. The councils are sometimes called
Whitley Councils.

See also ARBITRATION, CONCILIATION, INDUSTRIAL
COURT, INDUSTRIAL RELATIONS, WAGES COUNCILS, etc.

joint stock. The joint ownership by a group of people of a
business, or FIRM. The principle was understood and practised
even before the sixteenth century, but before the industrial
revolution there was little need for large amounts of CAPITAL.
Production was of a simple nature in general and whatever
monetary requirements that might arise could often be met by one
man, or a small group of men. By the nineteenth century, however, it was being found more and more difficult to raise funds
in this way and stock became owned jointly by larger and
larger numbers of people.

See COMPANIES and LIMITED LIABILITY.

joint supply. The SUPPLY of two or more ECONOMIC GOODS
which are produced together, eg beef, hide and glue; wool,
mutton and catgut; corn and straw. One product may be a BY-
PRODUCT of the other. See also COMPOSITE SUPPLY.

key currency. See RESERVE CURRENCY.

Keynesian Economics. The body of economic thought pro-
pounded by John Maynard (Lord) Keynes (1883–1946). Most of
Keynes' earlier work culminated in his *General Theory*, which is
fundamentally an examination of the determinants of the
general level of economic activity.

The starting point of the theory is the idea of *effective demand*
(see DEMAND), by which the amount of employment is trans
lated into terms of demand for goods, ie the eventual deter-
minant of the volume of employment is found in the degree to
which the ENTREPRENEUR decides to judge such employment
to be profitable. The total amount of money available to make
demand effective is the total money income created in the
economy. Payments are, of course, the obverse of receipts,
therefore NATIONAL INCOME equals NATIONAL OUTLAY and

employment can be seen to depend upon the size of national income.

Keynes established connections between employment consumption and investment, showing how a certain level of investment is needed to maintain income and consumption. If investment ceased altogether, for instance, this would mean a fall in total expenditure with the result that income and employment would fall. Consumption also would decline, further reducing income and, again, consumption until all income is used for consumption. This would be the lowest possible level of investment, ie zero, and it would be an equilibrium level of income and consumption.

The older approach to INTEREST was to regard it as equating savings and investment, but in Keynesian theory they are always equal. Saving is defined as income minus consumption ($S = Y - C$, where Y represents income) and we have seen that income equals consumption plus investment ($Y = C + I$), therefore investment equal savings ($I = S$). This conclusion has been much disputed, but is now largely accepted with minor modifications.

Another vital point in the Keynesian system is the relationship between the MARGINAL EFFICIENCY OF CAPITAL and the rate of interest, the two determinants of the level of investments. When an economy is emerging from a depression, ie 'revival', and business optimism and confidence is returning, investment increases because the marginal efficiency of capital (ie the rate of profit) is rising. Eventually this rise will cease and the marginal efficiency will fall. This accounts for fluctuations in the level of investment and subsequent fluctuations in the level of employment. This subsequent effect is subject to what Keynes called a *multiplier* action. The multiplier is the ratio between an increase in consumption and an increase in income. A change in income leads to a change in investment, which itself will generate a change in income.

See also ACCELERATOR, LEAKAGE and PROPENSITY TO INVEST.

kurtosis. This is the extent to which a DISTRIBUTION 'peaks'. A distribution with a marked peak is *leptokurtic* and one with a flat top *platykurtic*. The NORMAL CURVE is *mesokurtic*.

labour. The FACTOR OF PRODUCTION comprising all human economic effort, mental and physical, skilled or unskilled, applied to the PRODUCTION of WEALTH (ie creation of UTILITY) and in receipt of reward for the effort. See DIVISION OF LABOUR, MOBILITY and WAGES.

labour relations. See INDUSTRIAL RELATIONS.

labour theory of value. This theory states that the value of an

ECONOMIC GOOD derives solely from the amount of LABOUR embodied in it. Labour is, therefore, considered as the source and measure of value.

Of those to uphold the theory after Adam Smith, Marx developed it most fully and incorporated it in his attack upon CAPITALISM. Ricardo also expounded the theory, but refined it into the COST OF PRODUCTION THEORY OF VALUE, the criticisms of which apply equally to the labour theory.

See also UTILITY and VALUE.

labour turnover. The number of workers who leave a FIRM compared with the number engaged to replace them during a specific period of time.

laissez faire. 'Laissez faire et laissez-passer' (let things continue without interference). Domestically, this principle meant non-interference in the employment of people or the determination of prices in order that the individual might follow his own self-interest, unhampered by restrictions. These conditions existed in large measure in Britain in the early nineteenth century, but led to such distress and abuse that much legislation has since been enacted to eradicate for ever the social evils set in train by laissez faire doctrines.

land. One of the traditional FACTORS OF PRODUCTION: the one which embraces all natural resources, the original raw material for PRODUCTION. It can be defined as all that is a 'free gift of nature' and useful to man. This would include air, climate, fields, forests, deposits of minerals, fishing grounds, the sea itself and even the sun and moon. The definition includes FREE GOODS.

A more satisfactory definition might limit the free and useful gifts of nature to those which are scarce and can be made subject to a transaction of some kind.

large-scale production. The PRODUCTION of goods on a large scale, ie in large quantities. A FIRM increases its CAPACITY, or scale of production, by increases in the amounts of FACTORS OF PRODUCTION it employs, notably CAPITAL and LABOUR, and by increases in the efficiency of its factors, eg by DIVISION OF LABOUR.

Large-scale production has certain advantages; these are of an 'external' or 'internal' nature. That is, those which are enjoyed not only by the firm itself but also by the INDUSTRY; and those beneficial to the firm alone.

Large-scale production and *mass production* are often used interchangeably, but a significant difference should be noted. The former does not refer specifically to the manner of production and considerable variety, or individuality, of products may exist. Mass production, however, means the making of standardised products and the reduction of variety to the minimum.

See also RETURNS TO SCALE and SMALL-SCALE PRODUCTION.

law of diminishing returns. This is known variously as the law of *increasing costs*, of *non-proportional returns*, of *diminishing marginal productivity* and of *diminishing marginal revenue productivity*.

It is an ECONOMIC LAW that deals with the result of combining FACTORS OF PRODUCTION together in different proportions. Shackle has defined the law as follows: 'as the number of units of a variable factor employed in combination with given quantities of other factors is increased, the extra amount of product resulting from a unit increase in the variable factor (ie the marginal product), will, after a certain point, progressively decline.'

See DIMINISHING PRODUCTIVITY and RETURNS TO SCALE.

leads and lags. A term often used loosely in connection with overseas trade to cover all those temporary and abnormal influences affecting the BALANCE OF PAYMENTS (see also GOLD AND CONVERTIBLE CURRENCY RESERVE), but not easily isolated and measured. More precisely, 'leads and lags' indicate a displacement from normal in the time at which settlement is made in the course of INTERNATIONAL TRADE.

leakage. A term sometimes used to describe tendencies for CAPITAL FORMATION not to exert its full effect upon the NATIONAL INCOME.

legacy duty. See DEATH DUTIES.

legal tender. Any form of MONEY which is a legal quittance of a debt, ie money which, according to law, must be accepted as payment of any obligation stated in monetary terms.

lender of last resort. See BANK OF ENGLAND and PUBLIC WORKS LOANS BOARD.

letter of credit. An order in writing from a banker to his agent abroad, or to a banker abroad, to authorise payment to the person named in the letter of a specific sum, or amounts not in total exceeding that sum.

limited liability. When applied to COMPANIES this term refers to the principle whereby a shareholder cannot be held personally liable for a company's debts beyond the fully paid-up value of the SECURITIES he holds. If there is any unpaid-up portion (see CALL) the shareholder may be called upon to pay this.

limited partnership. A type of PARTNERSHIP in which the principle of LIMITED LIABILITY is extended to the holdings of non-active partners in the enterprise.

liquid. If something is 'liquid' it is easily converted into cash without appreciable loss in value. Liquid ASSETS, the most liquid being cash and bank deposits, are clearly the opposite of 'illiquid', or FROZEN, assets such as buildings and land, which may be difficult to sell quickly without loss in value.

Liquidity may also be used to denote ability to meet financial obligations in cash or its equivalent.

See also LIQUIDITY PREFERENCE

liquidation. The dissolution, or winding-up, of a business, ie the conversion of its ASSETS into cash, the settlement of any indebtedness there may be and the distribution among the owners of any funds remaining.

liquidity preference. This refers to the degree to which individuals prefer their funds to be near cash. They may prefer to hold savings in a completely liquid form, that is, as cash. Or, they may decide to accept a degree of 'illiquidity', that is, invest their savings. This latter choice implies reward to the saver-investor and the reward, in general, is greater the more illiquid the ASSETS are. The reward is INTEREST. See KEYNESIAN ECONOMICS.

liquidity ratio. In Britain this term is virtually restricted to the CLEARING BANKS, but it is largely synonymous with CASH RATIO, under which heading the principle is explained.

The RADCLIFFE REPORT said 'Having regard to their liquidity requirements the banks have gradually settled to the convention that their most liquid assets (cash, call money and bills discounted) should not fall below 30 per cent of their total "deposits" (the total of current, deposit and other accounts). Since October 1963, the minimum ratio has been 28 per cent.

local authority loans market. Local authorities in Britain are only able to finance 'capital investment' out of revenue to a very limited extent. They borrow the rest by the following methods:
  (i) by issuing SECURITIES;
  (ii) by short-term (unsecured) borrowing;
  (iii) by issuing short- or long-term MORTGAGES; and
  (iv) by using the facilities of the PUBLIC WORKS LOANS BOARD.

localisation or location of industry. The tendency for an industry to be located in a certain area, ie the SPECIALISATION of an area.

Such specialisation takes place for one or more reasons: eg suitable climate; presence of raw materials, fuel, labour, etc.; existence of satisfactory transport and communications facilities; proximity of a market; and 'industrial inertia', that is, the continuance of an industry in an area after the original cause has ceased to be effective.

In addition to the above one should note that government policy may well serve to locate an industry in a specified area (see DEPRESSED AREAS, etc).

lock-out. An industrial dispute in which the employer closes down the FIRM in an attempt to bring the workers to terms. See STRIKES.

London Bankers' Clearing House. This CLEARING HOUSE is controlled by the Committee of the London CLEARING BANKS. It deals with cheques paid into a branch of one clearing bank which are payable at a branch of another clearing bank.

See also BANKERS' CLEARINGS.

London Commodity Exchange. This is located at Plantation House in the City of London. The exchange originated in 1811 and is a market dealing in a wide range of commodities including rubber, sugar, cocoa, jute, pepper, spices, oilseeds and ivory.

London Foreign Exchange Market. This is a freely competitive FOREIGN EXCHANGE market comprising some 120 banks in London (British Commonwealth and foreign), all authorised by the Treasury as 'dealers in foreign exchange' (see AUTHORISED DEALER and EXCHANGE CONTROL).

Dealings take place by telephone, cable and telex.

London's wholesale food markets. A large proportion of Britain's home-produced produce is sent to the great distributing centres in London. London is a commercial focus point, very convenient for collection and distribution and directly serves a large population.

For horticultural produce Covent Garden and Spitalfields are the largest, with Borough, Stratford, Brentford and Greenwich: Smithfield is mainly for meat and Leadenhall for meat and poultry; Billingsgate for fish; King's Cross and Somers Town for potatoes; Islington market is for Kosher meat; and the Corn Exchange deals, of course, with cereal and cereal products.

long-dated. long-period. long-run. long-term. 'Long' is often used very loosely in economics without specific reference to any particular length of time. In the theory, this may be convenient because reference is being made to a significant change in conditions which cannot occur swiftly. For example, if short-term is defined as a period of time in which the supply of at least one FACTOR OF PRODUCTION is fixed, then, clearly, long-run, period, term, etc must be any term long enough for the supply of all factors to be variable. Also, it might be the length of time it takes an entrepreneur to realise his best output; and so on. Long-dated SECURITIES usually have a life of over fifteen years.

loss leader. A retail good priced below its ordinary level to attract customers who, it is hoped, will also buy normally priced merchandise.

macroeconomics. That part of the subject dealing with broad aggregates of economic entities; eg total production, consumption, employment, income, general price level, etc. Macroeconomics is not concerned with the detailed workings of an economy, which are investigated by MICROECONOMICS. See also ECONOMICS.

making-up. A term used in the STOCK EXCHANGE for the making-up of ACCOUNTS, which takes place on the first day of the SETTLEMENT. Making-up prices are fixed by the Council of the Stock Exchange to facilitate settlement.

managed money. A 'managed currency' system is one where the amount of MONEY is regulated arbitrarily by the authorities in order to achieve some objective, such as the stabilisation of the price level.

margin. In the commercial and financial sense, an extra amount beyond that necessary, a precautionary additional amount, etc. It is also the additional cover for speculative investments in which sense the STOCKBROKER provides that part of the cost of the investments which is not financed by the investor and the margin is the difference between the amount of the loan and the current value of the SECURITIES deposited as COLLATERAL SECURITY for the loan. This is 'buying on margin'.
In economic theory, the concept of the margin is of great importance in the analysis of changed conditions. The margin is a unitary change, increase or decrease, in an economic aggregate. Marginal analysis enables us to consider a situation, for example the quantity of fixed and variable FACTORS OF PRODUCTION employed by a firm and the possible consequences of marginal variations in the proportions of those factors.

marginal capital-output ratio. The amount of additional CAPITAL believed to be required to provide for an increase of one unit per annum in the real NATIONAL PRODUCT.

marginal cost. The additional increase in total COST resulting from the production of one more unit of output.

marginal efficiency of capital. Most CAPITAL is long-lasting and the entrepreneur can compute the *expected* returns from it; he can estimate the future annual returns, ie 'marginal revenue productivity'. The price he has to pay to borrow the money capital is the rate of INTEREST, and the problem is to compare this with future returns. If the prospective returns from the capital, discounted at the rate of interest payable on the money capital needed to buy the capital equipment, have a present value greater than the cost of the equipment, then it will pay to invest. The process of 'discounting' enables us to compare costs with expected returns, that is, to compare two rates—the necessary rate of discount and the rate of interest on the loan. The rate of discount which equates present value and present cost is the 'marginal efficiency of capital'.

See KEYNESIAN ECONOMICS.

marginal land. The last unit of land worth cultivating, that is, land which will just repay the cost of producing anything from it at ruling market prices. Also called 'margin of profitable cultivation'.

marginal producer. A producer who is just in business, that is, he is just able to meet his costs of production at the prevailing prices. See NORMAL PROFIT and PRODUCER'S RENT.

marginal product. The increase in total output that results from the use of one more increment of a variable FACTOR OF PRODUCTION in conjunction with other fixed factors.

marginal productivity. The ability of one more unit of a variable FACTOR OF PRODUCTION to increase total output when used in conjunction with other, fixed, factors.

marginal productivity theory of wages. Because of DIMINISHING PRODUCTIVITY it is argued that after a certain point an additional unit of LABOUR employed will only add to total output the value of the WAGES paid to that unit. The next unit would add less than the wage received and so would not be employed. The total amount of labour employed, therefore, is determined by the contribution made by and the wage paid to that last unit. Since the units are assumed to be identical and interchangeable, then the wage paid to the last employable (marginal) unit is the wage paid to all. However, this assumes too much for it to be of any practical significance. It assumes PERFECT COMPETITION, complete MOBILITY of labour and FULL EMPLOYMENT. Economists do not claim that the theory is a complete explanation, but that it 'throws into clear light the action of one of the causes that govern wages' (Marshall).

See WAGE-FUND THEORY.

marginal rate of substitution. In the *theory of consumer choice*, the economist reduces the actual range of choice to a 'two-good economy' in order to examine how an individual might react when selecting different combinations of these two commodities. If we assume, as in 'indifference analysis' (see INDIFFERENCE CURVE), that it is possible for the consumer to select different combinations of the two goods which yield the same satisfaction (or total UTILITY), then we can determine the rate at which one good is substituted for the other. That is, the quantity of one commodity or service that is required to compensate the consumer for the loss of one unit of the other commodity or service. This is the *marginal rate of substitution.*

marginal return to capital. The return to the investor on the investment of one additional unit of CAPITAL.

marginal revenue. The increase in total revenue resulting from the sale of one more unit of output.

marginal utility. See UTILITY.

market. Benham described this as 'any area over which buyers and sellers are in such close touch with one another, either directly or through dealers, that the prices obtainable in one part of the market affect the prices paid in other parts'.
Communication in a market may be by telephone, telegraph, telex, cable or radio; in which cases the market may well be world-wide. The wider and more perfect a market is the greater will be the tendency for the same price to rule at the same time for the same commodity.
See COMPETITION, IMPERFECT COMPETITION, PERFECT COMPETITION, etc.

marketing boards. These are CARTEL-like organisations set up to assist producers in the marketing of their products. In Britain, a number of such boards have been established in the agricultural field (milk, eggs, hops, wool).

market price or value. Under conditions of PERFECT COMPETITION, the market price is that at which the amount of a good or service offered by sellers just equals the quantity that will be accepted by the buyers. This must be qualified by stating that it occurs in a specific market and at a certain time. When these quantities are unequal, that is, SUPPLY is greater than DEMAND, or vice versa, then the market price will be lower, or higher, respectively. See also MARKET VALUATION, NORMAL PRICE and PRICE.

market trend. The general, long-term movement of prices of SECURITIES in the STOCK EXCHANGE.

market valuation. An assessment in a MARKET of the worth of something. When used in the STOCK EXCHANGE, it refers to the current price of SECURITIES, usually in contrast to their NOMINAL VALUE.

mark-up. The GROSS PROFIT that an article would yield if sold at the normal, or expected price. Or, the difference between the total cost of production and the selling price, ie the cost of distribution.

mass production. See LARGE-SCALE PRODUCTION.

mathematical economics. The analysis of economic data and the expression of principles and arguments by mathematical symbols and methods.

maturity. When applied to COMMERCIAL BILLS and SECURI-TIES, the date on which repayment of the PRINCIPAL is due.

mean deviation. This measure of DISPERSION is obtained by taking the ARITHMETIC MEAN of the differences (or deviations) of individual values from their average. The average may be either the arithmetic mean or the MEDIAN and all the deviations are taken to be positive.

mean variation. See MEAN DEVIATION.

median. This is the value of the mid-point of a DISTRIBU-TION; that is, there are as many values greater than it as there are values smaller.
See ARRAY and CENTRAL TENDENCY.

mediation. The act of coming between two parties in dispute in order to assist settlement; akin to ARBITRATION or CONCILIA-TION. See also COLLECTIVE BARGAINING, etc.

medium-dated. 'mediums'. SECURITIES with a life of between five and fifteen years. See also LONG- and SHORT-DATED.

medium of exchange. See MONEY.

memorandum of association. A document required from every joint-stock company (see JOINT STOCK and COMPANIES) at the time of its formation, stating its powers, objects and conditions of incorporation.

merchant bank. This name is used to describe a large number of financial institutions in the City of London. The origins of most of them are in the ordinary buying and selling of goods; business to which has been added a range of financial services, including ACCEPTANCE. Merchant banks tend to specialise in certain classes of business, but nearly twenty of them have made the acceptance of COMMERCIAL BILLS a vital part of their activities. These should be more strictly described as ACCEPT-ANCE HOUSES.
The merchant banks all do other business: some are active in the London Gold Market, the LONDON FOREIGN EXCHANGE MARKET, in merchanting, and some are also ISSUING HOUSES. All do some ordinary banking business, a substantial part of their deposits coming from other banks and companies abroad. They are domestic bankers only on a small scale, but they play an important role in the London MONEY MARKET. Like the joint-stock banks, insurance companies and some other institutions, the merchant banks act as trustees and as investment advisers.

merger. As explained under INTEGRATION, the term 'merger' is virtually interchangeable with several others, all of which refer to the joining together of two or more companies.
The advantages of a merger are: economies in capital expendi-

ture and in the use of current assets; easier access to the capital market; saving in overhead expenses; diversification; maintenance of selling price; greater funds available for advertising and research, etc. The disadvantages include the possible loss of a trade name and the personal touch; personality problems; inconvenience and expense; etc.

In addition to CARTEL, TRUST, etc, see LARGE-SCALE PRODUCTION.

microeconomics. The part of ECONOMICS concerned with the detailed workings of the economy, that is, the study of particular cases, such as the supply of butter, unemployment in the shipping industry, the best output for a firm, etc. See MACROECONOMICS.

minimum wage. A minimum wage level, usually established by law, to be paid to the employees in certain occupations or industries. The minimum may be agreed upon as the result of COLLECTIVE BARGAINING.

mint. A place where coins are made; usually operated by, or approved by, the State.

mixed economy. An ECONOMY containing the characteristics of both CAPITALISM and SOCIALISM that is, a combination of private and public ownership of the means of production, with some measure of control by the central government.

mobility. The degree of mobility possessed by FACTORS OF PRODUCTION is determined by the ease, or otherwise, with which they can change from one use to another or from one place to another. The extreme cases are 'perfect mobility', and 'immobility' (in which no change is possible).

Mobility in relation to employment is sometimes called 'economic mobility' and subdivided into *lateral*, performing the same task but in a different firm, or department of a firm; and *vertical*, performing a different task.

The commonest use of the term, however, is in the geographical sense, ie the movement from place to place. LAND is physically immobile, but has economic mobility and thus has limited SPECIFICITY. All other factors are mobile to some extent.

mode. This is the value of the most frequent score in a DISTRIBUTION. See BIMODAL and CENTRAL TENDENCY.

model. A mathematical system used to describe the workings of part or the whole of an economy.

monetary policy. This refers to the use of certain monetary controls by a government to regulate economic activity. They include restriction or expansion of the supply of MONEY and manipulation of the INTEREST rates in order to make borrowing

cheaper or dearer, or easier or more difficult to obtain. See
BANK RATE, OPEN MARKET OPERATIONS, SPECIAL DEPO-
SITS, etc.

money. Money is a commodity accepted by common consent
as a means of exchange, a medium in which prices are expressed,
a circulating medium to facilitate exchange and measure
WEALTH. It is possible to distinguish four major functions performed by money.

First: a 'medium of exchange', an intermediate selected commodity, whereby goods and services are paid for and debts and
other contracts discharged.

Second: a measure of value, a unit of account, a common
denominator of value in which records are kept, costs calculated,
and prices stated.

Third: a 'standard for deferred payments', that is, a basis for
credit transactions so that when payment is to be made at a future
date the exact extent of the obligation is known.

Fourth: a store of value or 'reserve of ready purchasing power',
that is, a means of conserving purchasing power.

Money can take numerous forms; historically, many commodities have performed the above functions but all have had to
be relatively scarce and universally wanted. The principal forms
of money now are coinage, notes and credit instruments.

See also BARTER, BANK MONEY, CONVERTIBILITY, FIAT
MONEY, FIDUCIARY ISSUE, etc.

money at call and short notice. *Call loan, call money,* or *money
at call,* all refer to short-period loans made by the banks in
Britain to the DISCOUNT HOUSES and, perhaps, to stock
JOBBERS.

money capital. See CAPITAL.

money market. A market that facilitates the borrowing and
lending of short-term funds (ie two to three years to MATURITY).
For a money market to exist there must be a supply of tempor-
arily idle funds seeking short-term INVESTMENT in an earning
ASSET. There must also exist a demand for temporary available
cash, either by the banks, etc, for the purpose of adjusting their
LIQUIDITY positions, or by the government when it decides to
finance itself by adding to the FLOATING DEBT or by issuing
short-dated BONDS.

Monopolies Commission. Under the Monopolies and Restrictive Practices (Inquiry and Control) Act of 1948, the Monopolies and Restrictive Practices Commission was established to
investigate cases referred to it by the Board of Trade. By 1956,
the commission had investigated twenty industries, including:
dental goods; electric lamps; motor-car tyres; linoleum; cathode
ray tubes; and had also carried out a wide enquiry into certain

practices under the heading 'collective discrimination'. In seventeen of the twenty industries investigated, the commission found conditions contrary to the 'public interest', although there has never been really clear guidance as to what this term means.

In 1956, the Restrictive Trade Practices Act was passed making illegal the collective enforcement of RESALE PRICE MAINTENANCE by groups of manufacturers and making compulsory the registration of all collective agreements relating to prices, conditions of supply, and manufacturing processes. See REGISTRAR OF RESTRICTIVE TRADING AGREEMENTS etc. The 1956 Act narrowed the commission's field of reference and changed its name to the Monopolies Commission. Out of the twenty-five cases examined up to 1964, only two 'cease and desist' orders were issued: in the cases of the supply of dental goods and imported timber. In 1965, the Monopolies and Mergers Act enlarged (to twenty-five) and reorganised the commission, and improved and extended the government's power to take action on the commission's reports.

monopolistic competition. See IMPERFECT COMPETITION.

monopoly. In economic theory, the most extreme departure from PERFECT COMPETITION is monopoly, which assumes a MARKET in which there is only one seller of a commodity. That is, where there is single control over the supply of a good or service and that control can be maintained.

In practice, 'pure' monopolies only rarely exist; for the purposes of the MONOPOLY COMMISSION'S investigations industries are monopolistic when at least one-third of the supply process or export of goods are controlled

(a) by one person (a firm or group of companies);
(b) by a restrictive agreement between firms; or
(c) by firms which so conduct their affairs as to limit competition.

See also BUYER'S MONOPOLY, DUOPOLY, IMPERFECT COMPETITION, NATURAL MONOPOLY, OLIGOPOLY, QUASI MONOPOLY, etc.

monopsony. See BUYER'S MONOPOLY.

mortgage. A mortgage is a conditional conveyance of land or other property as security for the performance of some condition, eg the payment of a debt; becoming void once the condition has been performed. That is, on repayment of the debt, the property is reconveyed to the debtor.

most-favoured-nation clause. An agreement, in a commercial treaty between countries, that they will confer on each other trade concessions that either may subsequently grant to any other country. See GENERAL AGREEMENT ON TARIFFS AND TRADE, etc.

multilateral. An agreement between more than two countries whereby they trade with each other, but do not pair for purposes of BALANCE OF PAYMENTS or TRADE. The existence of QUOTAS and TARIFFS do not, of themselves, impede multilateralism, although they may well reduce the volume of INTERNATIONAL TRADE.

See also BILATERALISM.

multimodal. See BIMODAL.

multiplier. See INDUCED CONSUMPTION and KEYNESIAN ECONOMICS.

National Board for Prices and Incomes. Early in 1965, the government decided to disband the National Incomes Commission and replace it with a National Board. The NBPI was set up in April and in the following months began to examine particular cases to advise the government whether or not the behaviour of prices, wages, salaries and other developments affecting money incomes were in the national interest.

national capital. See NATIONAL WEALTH.

National Debt. This is the debt of a central government incurred by expenditure which could not be met out of revenue. (When combined with the debts of local government, the total is sometimes called the 'public debt'.) This expenditure may be for productive purposes, such as the building of bridges, railways, harbours, roads, etc, or for unproductive purposes, such as war.

In Britain, the national debt now stands at about £30,000 million, incurred largely as a result of warfare.

The national debt consists of three parts:

(i) the FUNDED DEBT;
(ii) the FLOATING DEBT; and
(iii) the 'unfunded debt' (often classified with the floating debt because both are of a short-term character) which is made up of loans repayable on or before a specified date (war loan, defence bonds, etc.)

National Debt Commissioners. The Commissioners were first constituted in 1786 to apply SINKING FUNDS for the reduction of the NATIONAL DEBT. They have other duties relating to the investment and financial management of most of the large government funds; these include the POST OFFICE SAVINGS BANK Fund, the Fund for Bank for Savings (the TRUSTEE SAVINGS BANK), and the National Insurance Fund.

National Defence Bonds. See NATIONAL SAVINGS.

National Economic Development Council. The NEDC, or 'Neddy', was set up in 1962 as part of the British government's plans to secure economic stability and sustained growth. It was 'charged with the responsiblity of co-ordinating all the major expansion plans of British Industry' and its tasks include an examination of the economic performance of the nation with particular concern for 'plans for the future' in both the private and public sectors; a consideration of 'obstacles to economic growth' and the use of resources, and the seeking of agreement upon ways of increasing the rate of sound growth, competitive power and efficiency.

In March 1964, the formation was announced of the first five of the seventeen planned Economic Development Committees (the 'little Neddies') to cover the chemicals, chocolate and sugar confectionery, electronics, machine tools, and paper and board industries. Later committees were concerned with distributive trades, electrical engineering and wool textiles.

national income. The total net earnings received by the FACTORS OF PRODUCTION (ie WAGES + PROFIT + INTEREST + RENT) for their productive effort in an economy and for a specific period of time. This is also called 'national income at factor cost'.

A national income figure which has not had allowances for DEPRECIATION deducted is called the 'gross national income'. Once deducted, the figure is 'net national income'. In the early 1960s, the British gross national income was of the order of £25,000 million.

See NATIONAL OUTLAY and NATIONAL PRODUCT.

nationalisation. The public ownership and control of industry formerly owned by private interests.

In Britain, the scope of this state participation was greatly extended by the Nationalisation Acts of 1946–1949. As a result of these, the undertakings taken under government direction include the coal mines, railways, waterways, a section of civil aviation, gas, electricity, part of road transport, and the BANK OF ENGLAND.

National Joint Advisory Council. The need for closer and more regular consultation between employers, workers and the government was met by the establishment of the NJAC in October 1939. It was to be composed of representatives from the British Employer's Confederation and the TRADES UNION CONGRESS under the chairmanship of the Minister of Labour 'to advise the government on matters in which employers and workers have a common interest'.

The council has examined and advised on many important employment and INDUSTRIAL RELATIONS problems, eg AUTOMATION, recruitment and training of young workers, and the establishment of joint consultative machinery in industry (see NATIONAL PRODUCTION ADVISORY COUNCIL ON INDUSTRY). See also INDUSTRIAL COURT, etc.

national outlay. Both NATIONAL INCOME and NATIONAL PRODUCT are equivalent to national expenditure or outlay, which consists of the total expenditure of the community on the consumption of commodities and services plus sums used for CAPITAL FORMATION.

National Plan. In 1965, the British government published its 'national plan'. The plan was worked out with the assistance of the NATIONAL ECONOMIC DEVELOPMENT COUNCIL and in close consultation with industry. The basic objectives were to achieve a 25 per cent growth in NATIONAL PRODUCT by 1970 and, in so doing, increase prosperity for all and bring about a permanent improvement in our BALANCE OF PAYMENTS position.

national product. The value of the goods and services produced by an economy during a given period. As the product of a producing unit in a given period must be of exactly the same value as the sum of the incomes of the FACTORS OF PRODUCTION which gave rise to that product, then national product must equal NATIONAL INCOME. These are also equal to the NATIONAL OUTLAY as the total expenditure on the consumption of commodities and services plus sums expended on capital goods must equal both the total product and the total incomes.

National Production Advisory Council on Industry. This body is separate from the NATIONAL JOINT ADVISORY COUNCIL; it serves as a forum for the government to consult national and regional representatives on government policy and procedure, where these affect industrial production.

national savings. Savings sponsored by the central government. In Britain, the POST OFFICE SAVINGS BANK and the TRUSTEE SAVINGS BANKS were both well established in the nineteenth century and during the first world war the War Savings Committee was set up by the government to promote an official savings drive. At the same time, the National Savings Certificate was introduced as a new type of long-term SECURITY, encashable at PAR at any time, with interest payable only on encashment, but free of income tax.

Current national savings securities are:
the National Savings Certificate;
the five-year National Development Bonds, which replaced the Defence Bonds (first issued in 1939 and repayable at par or on notice, interest being paid half-yearly and taxable); and the Premium Savings Bonds, first issued in 1956, giving their buyers a chance to win prizes from £25 upwards.

national wealth. The total value, in monetary terms, of all the economic goods possessed by the members of an economy at a specified time. The national wealth would, therefore, exclude economic goods owned by foreigners. The expression 'national capital' is sometimes used as an alternative.

natural monopoly. A MONOPOLY due either to natural circumstances, or to the characteristics inherent in a FIRM. In the first case, for instance, a particular area of land may have a quality which will produce a crop that cannot be produced anywhere else. In the second, COMPETITION may be contrary to the public interest, or self-destructive.

natural resources. This term is identical in meaning with that of LAND, that is, the WEALTH freely supplied by nature.

negotiable instrument. This has been defined as an instrument 'the property in which is acquired by anyone who takes it bona fide and for value, notwithstanding any defect of title in the person from whom he took it'. A test of 'negotiability' is to determine whether the property in the instrument can be acquired in good faith through a theft. If it can, the instrument is negotiable.
Thus, in certain circumstances, a COMMERCIAL BILL is negotiable, while a BILL OF LADING, although it is transferable, is not negotiable.

net. Clear of all charges or deductions; not GROSS.

net advantages. A phrase used to denote the general advantages of an occupation. Some of those involved are a sense of vocation, length of holidays, congeniality of the work, environment, social prestige, security and regularity of employment, opportunity to supplement normal earnings, payments in kind, etc.
See FRINGE BENEFITS and WAGES.

net assets. The ASSETS attributable to the share capital (see CAPITAL) after deducting external liabilities including the future taxation reserve (see TAX RESERVE CERTIFICATE) and the NOMINAL VALUE of any DEBENTURES, added to any PREMIUM payable on them and any arrears of INTEREST.

net asset worth. A measurement of the value of ordinary shares (see SECURITIES), which is calculated by dividing the NET EQUITY ASSETS by the number of such shares.

net equity assets. The NET ASSETS minus the repayment value of the preference capital (see SECURITIES) including any arrears of preference DIVIDEND.

net investment. INVESTMENT after providing for DEPRECIATION and the replacement of CAPITAL.

net national debt. The total NATIONAL DEBT after deducting that part of it held by the government in SINKING FUNDS, etc.

net profit. The residue left from GROSS PROFIT after the deduction of selling and operating expenses (including DEPRE-CIATION charges, auditors' and directors' fees, interest payments, etc). See also PROFIT and TURNOVER.

net profit margin. NET PROFIT expressed as a percentage of TURNOVER.

new issue. The issue of SECURITIES which are offered to the public either directly, or through BROKERS, by companies themselves, or on their behalf by an ISSUING HOUSE. See also OFFER FOR SALE.

new issue market. A MARKET in NEW ISSUES. In Britain, the new issue market was once very active in overseas issues, but, since 1932, the emphasis has changed to domestic issues. See ISSUING HOUSE.

new time. The 'new time', which is also called the 'new account' or 'newgo', is the ACCOUNT in the STOCK EXCHANGE following the one in which dealing takes place. Transactions can be made for four days before SETTLEMENT ie 'new time dealings', to be settled at the end of the next account period.

nominal income. Money wages, nominal wages or nominal income is the actual amount, in monetary units, received as income. See REAL INCOME.

nominal value. This, also called nominal share value, is the FACE VALUE of SECURITIES, such as ordinary shares, preference shares, etc. See MARKET VALUATION.

nominal yield. The rate of return, usually expressed as a percentage, on SECURITIES calculated on their NOMINAL VALUE.

non-cumulative dividend. A DIVIDEND not paid when due to SHARE-HOLDERS, which does not become a liability of the company and need not be paid at a future date. See also ACCU-MULATIVE DIVIDEND, SECURITIES, etc.

non-proportional returns. See LAW OF DIMINISHING RE-TURNS.

non-resident account. Under the EXCHANGE CONTROL regula-tions, bank accounts held in Britain in sterling are classified according to the residence of the account holder. If he is per-manently resident outside the SCHEDULED TERRITORIES the account is a non-resident one.

normal curve. The normal or Gaussian curve (or distribution) is a very important symmetrical THEORETICAL DISTRIBUTION. Its mathematical properties are well known and are of great value in statistical method, particularly where SAMPLES are involved. For example, it is known that 68·26 per cent of the area (of the distribution) is encompassed by the range from one

STANDARD DEVIATION below the ARITHMETIC MEAN to one standard deviation above it.

See CENTRAL LIMIT THEOREM and STANDARD ERROR.

normal price. When the amount of a good or service offered by sellers in a MARKET is not equal to the quantity that will be accepted by buyers (ie DEMAND), then there will be a market price higher or lower than it would be if supply and demand were equal. The existence of a higher price may have the effect of either contracting demand or expanding supply, and vice versa, with the result that it can be assumed that eventually there will be an equilibrium between supply and demand. At this point, there will be an equilibrium, or normal, price, sometimes called normal value. See also SUPPLY AND DEMAND.

normal profit. A valuable concept in economic theory which enables us to consider a cost for the ENTREPRENEUR. Normal profit is the minimum income that the entrepreneur will accept, that is, the least reward he will accept in return for his entrepreneurial contribution to production. See PROFIT.

not negotiable. See NEGOTIABLE INSTRUMENT.

null hypothesis. This is the assumption that the true difference between two STATISTICS is zero and that any observed difference is due solely to chance. A SIGNIFICANCE test can then be made to see if the hypothesis should be approved or rejected.

occupational necessities. Those things necessary for the efficient performance of an occupation, eg a motor-car for a doctor, a teacher's books, etc.

offer. In the STOCK EXCHANGE, to 'offer' is to show that one has SECURITIES to sell at a given price. If the offer is made by a JOBBER, then the higher of the two prices he states is the 'offered price'.

offer for sale. An offer to the general public of SECURITIES, particularly shares in COMPANIES

See ISSUING HOUSE and NEW ISSUE.

official list. The list of dealings and prices in the STOCK EXCHANGE published at the end of each day's business.

official support. Buying by the BANK OF ENGLAND or some other agency for the government of CURRENCY (sterling in the LONDON FOREIGN EXCHANGE MARKET) or SECURITIES to support the MARKET PRICE. See EXCHANGE EQUALISATION ACCOUNT and OPEN MARKET OPERATIONS.

ogive. See CUMULATIVE FREQUENCY DISTRIBUTION.

oligopoly. A departure from PERFECT COMPETITION in which there are only a few producers of a good or service. The commodity produced may be homogeneous, in which case the oligopoly may be called 'perfect', or there may be PRODUCT DIFFERENTIATION, in which case the INDUSTRY may be called 'imperfect oligopoly'.

Oligopoly, like DUOPOLY is sometimes called 'partial monopoly'.

See also IMPERFECT COMPETITION and MONOPOLY.

open market operations. The buying or selling of SECURITIES in the open market by a CENTRAL BANK for the purpose of curtailing or expanding the volume of CREDIT. By selling securities the central bank can absorb funds, and by buying them it can release funds into the MONEY MARKET.

See 'BACK-DOOR' OPERATIONS, BANK OF ENGLAND, BANK RATE, GOVERNMENT BROKER, etc.

open shop. See CLOSED SHOP.

operating cost. See COSTS.

opportunity cost. This implies measuring the cost of anything in terms of the most desirable alternative, or gain, foregone. This notion can be applied to anything of economic significance. The opportunity or alternative cost of a house to society is the value of the next most useful goods that could have been produced with the FACTORS OF PRODUCTION used to build the house. The opportunity cost of a theatre ticket is the amount of satisfaction that could have been obtained had the money been spent on the next best thing. And so on.

opportunity curve. In a 'two-good economy', ie one in which choice is limited to two economic goods, it is possible for the price of one to be expressed in terms of the other (because the value of both can be measured independently in terms of money). Then, a certain amount of one is 'worth' a certain amount of the other. In the diagram explained under INDIFFERENCE CURVE, a line joining these two amounts is an opportunity curve, the amounts both representing how much the individual is able to buy with the funds available. The intermediate points on the line all represent combinations of the two economic goods the individual has the opportunity to obtain with these funds.

optimum. This is achieved when the most favourable economic conditions apply.

option. An agreement permitting one to choose whether to buy or sell something within a given time, in accordance with the terms of the agreement.

ordinary dividend. The DIVIDEND paid to the holder of ordinary shares (see SECURITIES).

ordinary shares. See SECURITIES.

Organisation for Economic Co-operation and Development. By 1960, the economic recovery of Europe from the Second World War was complete and it was becoming increasingly realised that the economic efforts being made on both sides of the Atlantic would have to be co-ordinated if the needs of the 'emergent nations' were to be met. The USA provided the initiative, and by April 1960, a plan had been drawn up for the replacement of the Organisation for European Economic Co-operation by a new body, viz the OECD.

The organisation came into existence in 1961 and its members undertook to pursue policies of economic growth, employment and a rising standard of living amongst themselves, while maintaining financial stability. They pledged themselves to contribute to economic expansion in all countries, and to the expansion of world trade on a non-discriminatory basis.

output. The amount of a good or service, or both, produced by a producing unit, that is, by a FIRM, an INDUSTRY or an ECONOMY.

over-capitalised. A FIRM is over-capitalised if its CAPITAL is greater than the scale of its operations requires. See UNDER-CAPITALISED.

overdraft. A loan facility granted by a bank to a customer, whereby he is permitted to draw upon his account (to overdraw) beyond the amount deposited therein and up to an agreed amount. See BANK CREDIT and CREDIT.

over-full employment. See FULL EMPLOYMENT.

overhead cost. See COSTS.

over-production. This occurs when more of a commodity or service is produced than is required for consumption. See PRODUCTION.

over-saving theory of the trade cycle. This is based upon the belief that the unequal distribution of the NATIONAL INCOME results in so great a volume of saving among those in the higher income groups that the investment which follows creates more productive capacity than is required in the economy. That is, there is OVER-PRODUCTION, UNEMPLOYMENT increases and a DEPRESSION develops (ie RECESSION). See TRADE CYCLE and UNDER-CONSUMPTION THEORY.

over-subscribed issue. An ISSUE for which applications to buy are in excess of SECURITIES available.

over-valued currency. An EXCHANGE RATE for a currency may be said to be in equilibrium when the SUPPLY of it equals the DEMAND for it. If, at a certain rate, supply exceeds demand in the long-run then the currency is said to be 'over-valued' and a downward pressure will exist on the value of that currency in terms of others.

paid-up capital. See CAPITAL.

paper money. MONEY in the form of paper documents issued by the government, or on governmental authority. See CONVERTIBILITY, FIAT MONEY, FIDUCIARY ISSUE and REDEEMABLE.

par. Equal; a term used when the price of SECURITIES (ie MARKET PRICE or VALUATION) is equal to the NOMINAL, or 'paid-up', VALUE.

parameter. This is a STATISTIC relating to a POPULATION.

par exchange rate. The price of one country's currency in terms of another as described by the INTERNATIONAL MONETARY FUND. The value of each currency is expressed in terms of gold and, from these valuations, the rates are obtained. Unlike the GOLD STANDARD, gold is merely used as a measuring unit.

parity. Equality; a 'parity of exchange' meaning the ratio at which things are exchangeable. The term is most used in connection with currencies, in which case it is an agreed, fixed EXCHANGE RATE for a currency around which limited fluctuations are usually allowed.

partial monopoly. See DUOPOLY and OLIGOPOLY.

participating preference share. See SECURITIES.

partly-paid. SECURITIES for which the full NOMINAL VALUE has not been paid and on which a liability to pay the balance exists (see *paid-up capital* under CAPITAL). See CALL, OFFER FOR SALE, etc.

partnership. A FIRM which has been created through a contractual arrangement between two or more people. Under the Companies Acts in Britain, the number of partners were limited to twenty, or, in the case of a banking concern, to ten. Partners have equal powers and responsibilities and each is jointly liable with his co-partners for all the debts and obligations of the firm. See COMPANIES, JOINT-STOCK and LIMITED PARTNERSHIP.

par value. This term is an alternative to PAR EXCHANGE RATE and, when applied to SECURITIES, to PAR.

passive trade balance. See UNFAVOURABLE TRADE BALANCE.

pegging. This term is used when an attempt is made to maintain a price or rate, or to keep it within close limits. The term is often applied to intervention in a FOREIGN EXCHANGE market by the authorities to restrict the movement of EXCHANGE RATES. See EXCHANGE EQUALISATION ACCOUNT and PARITY.

percentile. The percentile rank of a given value in an ARRAY is the percentage of values in the DISTRIBUTION below that value. For example, the 25th percentile is the lower QUARTILE. See DECILE.

perfect competition. An important concept in economic theory that acts as a limiting case, departures from which include DUOPOLY, IMPERFECT COMPETITION, MONOPOLY and OLIGOPOLY. Perfect competition is the opposite of monopoly and the market conditions necessary to satisfy it include:

(i) an unlimited number of buyers and sellers in each market so that the behaviour of any one has no appreciable significance for market price;

(ii) all buyers and sellers are fully informed of each other's intentions;

(ii) all factors of production are perfectly mobile and there is freedom of entry for new firms into all markets; and

(iv) all units of the same commodity are homogeneous and buyers are indifferent from whom they buy and sellers are indifferent to whom they sell.

perfect market. See MARKET.

perpetual debenture. A DEBENTURE with no MATURITY date, the INTEREST being paid indefinitely.

personal capital. See CAPITAL.

personal distribution. See DISTRIBUTION.

piecework. A method of paying WAGES, whereby payment depends upon the amount produced by the individual worker. This is also called 'payment by results' and it is a method that works by INCENTIVE unless, of course, the rate enables the worker to achieve his 'wage target' too easily.

placing. A method used to ISSUE SECURITIES. A 'private placing' means that the securities are sold by the BROKERS, who are making the placing for their clients (a 'placed' issue may never be quoted on the STOCK EXCHANGE).
See also INTRODUCTION, OFFER FOR SALE and NEW ISSUES.

plough back. The re-INVESTMENT of PROFITS made by COMPANIES in themselves, that is, the profit is not distributed, but used to buy capital goods (see CAPITAL) such as buildings, machinery, etc.

poisson distribution. A form of the BINOMIAL DISTRIBUTION in which the number of events is large and one of the two possible values each event may take is very unlikely.

population. The population or *universe*, is the totality of items in a statistical investigation. If all the items are used, the study is called a *census*; otherwise SAMPLES are taken.

portfolio. A list of SECURITIES.

Post Office Savings Bank. This was established in Britain in 1861 in order to facilitate the collection of savings, provide the safest possible custody, and to encourage saving by paying interest on the money deposited.

See also NATIONAL SAVINGS and TRUSTEE SAVINGS BANK.

post-war credits. These were enforced loans to the State, levied as part of INCOME TAX (see TAXATION) during the second world war, with the intention of making the refund after the war.

potential demand. A DEMAND expected at some future date. Eg if the power to purchase is increasing, or cuts in taxation are expected the 'potential' becomes 'effective demand'.

preference capital. Synonymous with preference shares—see SECURITIES.

preference shares. See SECURITIES.

preferential duty. See DISCRIMINATORY DUTY.

premium. A payment for INSURANCE cover; or a payment for a loan in lieu of, or in addition to, INTEREST; or the amount by which a currency or a SECURITY stands above its PAR VALUE or ISSUE price. That is, the excess of the MARKET PRICE over the PAR, or paid-up value of the securities. In the case of currency, it would be the excess of the market price (ie EXCHANGE RATE) over an official rate, or normally ruling rate.

price. An estimation of the value of an economic good in terms of MONEY. Prices are, of course, possible in a BARTER system, where no money exists. Under these circumstances, the price of a good or service is expressed in terms of another good or service, ie an EXCHANGE RATE. See MARKET PRICE, NORMAL PRICE, etc.

price discrimination. This occurs when it is possible to charge different prices to different groups or individuals for the same good or service. Such a pricing policy can succeed only if those who pay the higher price are unable to buy at the lower prices. Therefore, it follows that there must be control over the whole supply of the economic good. See MONOPOLY.
Price discrimination can occur where there is geographical separation of the MARKETS, for example, one country may attempt to increase its export trade by charging a lower price in the export market than in the home market for the same commodity. This is known as DUMPING.

price fixing. An administrative fixing of price level; also called 'price control'.

price guarantee. See SUPPORT.

price leader. Where COMPETITION exists in an industry it is possible that the majority of FIRMS follow a price determined by one, the 'leader'. Such a pricing policy may mean that the price level is higher than it would be if conditions were truly competitive. See MARKET PRICE, etc.

price system. This is an economic system in which PRICES are determined by the forces of the MARKET.

prime cost. See COSTS.

principal. MONEY on which INTEREST is paid.

prior charges. SECURITIES ranking before ordinary shares for CAPITAL repayment and INTEREST or DIVIDEND distribution, eg DEBENTURES and preference shares.

private capital. See CAPITAL.

private company. See COMPANY.

private enterprise. A feature of CAPITALISM in which economic activities are carried on with the expectation of PROFIT by private individuals or groups (see COMPANY, PARTNERSHIP, etc).

probability. The likelihood that a specific event will occur. In statistics, a numerical value is used to state probability, eg three chances in a thousand, 0·997 or 99·7 per cent.

probability distribution. A series of probabilities corresponding to all the values of the variable which are possible. It can be regarded as a frequency DISTRIBUTION standardised in such a way that the total frequency (ie number of values) is one.

producer. One whose activities result in PRODUCTION.

producer good. A capital good (see CAPITAL).

producer's capital. See CAPITAL.

producer's rent. The total COSTS of PRODUCTION for any output must normally be the minimum that the FIRM can receive as REVENUE and remain in business. It follows that for every ouput there must be a minimum PRICE at which the firm will BREAK-EVEN. If DEMAND for the firm's product is such that at one of these minimum prices it will just carry off the appropriate output, we say that no 'producer's rent' exists. This firm will be a MARGINAL PRODUCER.
Other firms in the INDUSTRY might be in more advantageous positions and have lower costs of production. These firms will, therefore, be earning a surplus, that is, 'producer's rent'.
See NORMAL PROFIT, PROFIT and RENT.

product. The result of PRODUCTION. See BY-PRODUCT.

product differentiation. The procedure whereby a PRODUCT is made to be, or seem to be, different from other products.

Differentiation may be based on certain characteristics of the product itself such as exclusive patented features; trade-marks; trade-names; peculiarities of the package or container; or singularity in quality, design, colour or style.

See COMPETITION, IMPERFECT COMPETITION, etc.

production. Fraser has defined this well: 'production for economic purposes must on the face of it consist, not in making or creating *things* (which is perhaps the meaning usually attached to the word in ordinary language) but in creating utility. Production in this sense *may*, of course, involve creating "things"—as when a manufacturer converts cotton thread into shirts; or gold ingots into pen nibs and wedding rings. But the making of things is as such irrelevant to economic production. For the economist all activities must be included which yield useful results, whether they are embodied in material objects or not. The boot-black who cleans my shoes is as much a "producer" as the cobbler who mends them or the manufacturer who makes them; the man who works in my garden is "producing" when he mows the lawn or weeds the border no less than when he grows strawberries for my tea. In one way or another all these forms of labour create *utility*.'

See UTILITY.

productivity. The amount produced by a FACTOR OF PRODUCTION in a given period of time; the efficiency with which productive resources are used; or the relationship between physical resources used in PRODUCTION and the units of output produced in a specified period of time.

See also MARGINAL PRODUCTIVITY.

profit. Profit is often regarded as the difference between the total expenses involved in making or buying something and the total revenue accruing from its sale. This difference could be interpreted as a return on CAPITAL and measured in various ways. For example, a year's profit could be related to the amount of capital used; or the profit could be stated as the proportion by which the price per unit sold was greater than the cost, that is, as a rate of TURNOVER. This interpretation may be useful commercially, but is of little use in economic theory in which profit is regarded as a source of income, with a flow measurable over time. In fact, a careful distinction has to be made between the meanings of profit to the economist and to others.

In accountancy, profit is a broad term defined rather as it is above. The difference between selling price and cost price is called GROSS PROFIT and found in the 'trading account'; and if expenses such as wages, rent, rates, lighting, etc are deducted, as in the 'profit and loss account', the remainder is called NET PROFIT. But, this net profit may contain a further cost element, the earnings of management, and the economist would insist that the profit was still *gross*.

Furthermore, gross profit may include what should strictly be termed INTEREST. A firm using borrowed capital regards the interest payable on this capital as an expense and excludes it from profit. Other firms using their own money capital include in profit the entire return on it. If the true net profit is to be isolated, it would be necessary to deduct from the gross return on capital the interest it would have earned if lent to someone else on good security. RENT also ought to be excluded by a firm possessing its own land or buildings.

Profit, then, is the residual reward received by the entrepreneur after all other payments to factors of production have been made. This is also called *pure profit*.

See NORMAL PROFIT.

profit-sharing. A system of remuneration of labour in which a bonus in proportion to net profits (in the commercial sense under PROFIT) is given in addition to WAGES.

promissory note. The Bills of Exchange Act, 1882, defines a promissory note as 'An unconditional promise in writing made by one person to another, signed by the maker, engaging to pay on demand, or at a fixed or determinable future time, a sum certain in money, to, or to the order of, a specified person or to bearer'. A promissory note is a NEGOTIABLE INSTRUMENT. See COMMERCIAL BILLS, etc.

propensity to invest. The relationship between total income and that part of income not devoted to consumer expenditure, is called the 'propensity to save' (see KEYNESIAN ECONOMICS). When there is equilibrium in the economy, savings equal investment, that is, the propensity to save is the same as the propensity to invest. But, when there is disequilibrium, the relationship between total income (ie NATIONAL INCOME) and that part of it spent on new CAPITAL FORMATION (ie the propensity to invest) may differ from the propensity to save. If investment is greater than savings, income tends to increase; and vice versa.

prospectus. A document, subject to strict legal requirements, in which details are given of SECURITIES to be offered for sale. See ISSUE, etc.

protection. The policy of imposing TARIFFS on imported goods in order to protect domestic industries. Some of the main arguments in favour of protection are:
  (i) that essential industries need protection, eg agriculture and those providing defence needs, to reduce dependence upon foreign sources in case of war;

(ii) Protection of an INFANT INDUSTRY;

(iii) UNEMPLOYMENT is reduced;

(iv) DUMPING is prevented; and

(v) BALANCE OF TRADE and PAYMENTS are improved.

See also COMPARATIVE ADVANTAGES, FREE TRADE, etc.

public company. See COMPANY.

public debt. See NATIONAL DEBT.

public finance. The financial operations of central and local government. See BUDGET, TAXATION, etc.

public good. An ECONOMIC GOOD supplied, without direct payment, to people by the government, eg parks, museums, libraries, education, etc.

public utility. An industry, such as gas, electricity, water and transport facilities, which requires heavy and highly specialised initial investment of capital, on which the return is slow. These are essential public services, the supply of which would not be necessarily forthcoming from private enterprise. See NATIONAL-ISATION.

public works. The building of roads, bridges, canals, public baths and parks, and other public construction projects designed to increase the welfare of the community. See INFRA-STRUC-TURE.

Public Works Loans Board. The first Commissioners of Public Works were appointed by an 1817 statute to make loans for PUBLIC WORKS. They were required to ensure that security was adequate, and that repayment be made in accordance with the MORTGAGE terms.

By and large, these requirements are still applicable.

The PWLB is financed by the Exchequer and must be regarded by the local authorities as a 'lender of last resort', to whom they can go if money cannot be borrowed at reasonable terms on the market (LOCAL AUTHORITY LOANS MARKET).

purchasing power parity. This exists when the EXCHANGE RATE between two currencies (both of which may be FIAT MONEY) is such that equivalent amounts of the currencies have identical purchasing powers in their respective countries. Assuming FREE TRADE and the absence of arbitrary national manipulation of currency, a 'purchasing power parity exchange rate' would preserve equilibrium.

The theory can be criticised because: the price level of goods not involved in international trade will not affect the rate of exchange; it is difficult, in practice, to compare purchasing power in different countries; it tends to ignore the effects in the FOREIGN

EXCHANGE market of changes in the supply of, and demand for, currencies; and there are influences of a speculative and political nature on the rates of exchange.

pure profit. See PROFIT.

pyramid, to. In the STOCK EXCHANGE, to continue buying a SECURITY when the price is rising. This establishes a higher MARKET PRICE. See AVERAGE, TO.

quadratic mean. The square root of the ARITHMETIC MEAN of the squares of the values.
See CENTRAL TENDENCY.

quality control. The use of statistical theory and techniques to record and check on the measurable qualities of products and processes.

quantity theory of money. This states that if a given quantity of MONEY exists for use as a medium of exchange and is sufficient to effect a certain volume of transactions at a certain level of PRICES, then an increase in the quantity will force up the price level for those transactions, assuming the number of them does not change.
However, a certain amount of money can effect more or less transactions in a given period of time, according to the speed with which it changes hands, ie its 'velocity of circulation'. If money circulates through the economic system twice as fast as before, this is equivalent to twice the quantity of money.
The theory is further refined to take account of BANK MONEY and its velocity of turnover, because such money is a significant proportion of the actual quantity of money.
The theory has several shortcomings. For example, care should be used in applying it to small or short-term fluctuations because it is possible for one change to be offset by another. Furthermore, if there are unemployed FACTORS OF PRODUCTION in the economy, an increase in the quantity of money may increase the level of production, thus using more resources and increasing the number of transactions, without a rise in price taking place.

quartile. The first, or lower, quartile has one quarter of the values in a DISTRIBUTION below it; the third, or upper, quartile has three quarters of the values below it. The second quartile is the MEDIAN.

quartile deviation. See SEMI-INTERQUARTILE RANGE.

quasi-monopoly. The possession of a complete MONOPOLY implies the control of all of the available supply of a certain economic good. In some cases, although no such complete control exists, the advantages are still so great that effective competition is virtually impossible. Such a situation is sometimes called a 'quasi-monopoly'. See also DUOPOLY, OLIGOPOLY, etc.

quasi-rent. See RENT.

quick asset. See ASSET (*floating asset*).

quotas. The allotment to individuals, firms or countries of maximum permitted quantities of goods. The term is frequently used in connection with imports, so that an 'import quota' is a quantitive restriction imposed on goods entering a country.
See FREE TRADE, GENERAL AGREEMENT ON TARIFFS AND TRADE, etc.

quotation. In the STOCK EXCHANGE this refers both to the privilege granted by the council of having the price of a SECURITY appear in the OFFICIAL LIST, and to the two prices quoted by the JOBBER, when he is approached by a STOCK-BROKER.

Radcliffe Report. In July 1959, the *Committee on the Workings of the Monetary System* made its report (the Radcliffe Report) on an inquiry into the working of the monetary and credit system.
The report is an abundant source of material and comment. It begins with a 'background of post-war monetary policy', in which the conditions of the 1950s are outlined.
The second chapter deals with 'The objectives of monetary policy' and it summarises the objectives in pursuit of which monetary measures may be used:
  (i) a high and stable level of employment;
 (ii) reasonable stability of the internal purchasing power of money;
(iii) steady economic growth and improvement of the standard of living;
 (iv) some contribution, implying a margin in the balance of payments, to the economic development of the outside world; and
  (v) a strengthening of London's international reserves, implying a further margin in the balance of payments.
Other chapters are descriptive: of the financing of the public sector; of the financial institutions in the private sector; and the work of the BANK OF ENGLAND.
The report also deals with questions of policy and with 'The influence of monetary measures', 'The management of the National Debt', and 'International aspects of the monetary system'.
The committee also concludes that it is the LIQUIDITY of the economy, rather than the supply of money, that the authorities should seek to influence in their attempts to control the pressure of demand.

Chapter VII looks at the problems of managing the NATIONAL DEBT, but it also deals with the technical arrangements for the issue of both bills and bonds, and for OPEN MARKET OPERATIONS in them.

This is followed by an enquiry into 'The status and organisation of the Bank of England'.

The final three chapters review the 'Statistics' available and how adequate they are for monetary policy.

random variable. A numerical VARIABLE which can take different values with different proportions.

range. A measure of DISPERSION that is simply the difference between the smallest and the largest values in a DISTRIBUTION.

rationalisation. A rather vague term for an increase in the efficiency of an industry. It has been described as 'a process necessary to produce higher organisation rather than to confer monopolistic advantages'.

raw material. A resource prior to PRODUCTION, during which process its nature is changed. For example, iron ore is a raw material that is transformed into steel. Then, steel is a raw material that is changed into refrigerators, etc.

real. The actual nature of something. See the following terms.

real income. As opposed to NOMINAL INCOME (the actual sum of MONEY received as income), real income refers to the purchasing power of that income. Real income thus takes into account changes in prices, ie in the value of money. See INDEX NUMBER.

real national income. real national product. The comparison of a country's NATIONAL INCOME (or PRODUCT) in one year with that of another year would produce a false picture if the general price level had changed from one year to the other. If the figures are adjusted to take account of changes in prices, ie in the value of money, then we have a 'real' comparison. See INDEX NUMBER.

recession. The term given to a falling-off in business activity. It could be a temporary phenomenon, but could continue into a DEPRESSION. See TRADE CYCLE.

reciprocity. The granting of concessions to a country in return for concessions granted by it.

The term is also used in connection with social security (see WELFARE STATE) benefits. Britain has reciprocal agreements on national insurance, industrial injuries and family allowances with several countries.

redeemable. Capable of being recovered, or freed, by payment. All debts are normally redeemable, as are most SECURITIES (redeemable preference shares, DEBENTURES, and most GOVERNMENT SECURITIES).

If something is 'irredeemable' then there is no prospect of repayment. This is true of some securities, eg some debentures and CONSOLS.

redeemable preference shares. See SECURITIES.

redemption. Recovery, usually by payment. The redemption of a debt is the repayment of the amount borrowed. The 're-demption date' is the date on which redemption must take place (see MATURITY).

redeployment. A rearrangement of FACTORS OF PRODUCTION, FIRMS, or INDUSTRIES so as to increase efficiency, ie for higher PRODUCTIVITY. See also RATIONALISATION.

rediscount. The discounting of something which has already changed hands at a DISCOUNT.

redundancy. This means the superabundance of a FACTOR OF PRODUCTION, product, etc. It is almost exclusively used to refer to LABOUR for which there is no employment, ie labour dis-missed for reasons other than misconduct.

Redundancy is sometimes called 'involuntary unemployment' (see UNEMPLOYMENT).

reflation. The use of DEFLATION or INFLATION to restore a previous price level, ie to restore a former value of the monetary unit.

Registrar of Restrictive Trading Agreements. The Restrictive Trade Practices Act of 1956 provided for the registration of *Restrictive Trading Agreements* (see RESTRICTIVE TRADE PRACTICES) and the judicial examination of such agreements (the RESTRICTIVE PRACTICES COURT). The Act requires the entry in a register of the particulars of a wide range of restrictive agreements and the Registrar is responsible for keeping the register and for bringing the agreements before the appropriate court. See also MONOPOLIES COMMISSION.

regression. This analysis attempts to establish the sort of re-lationship that might exist between two VARIABLES, so that values of one may be predicted from given values of the other. See CORRELATION.

rent. In ordinary usage, rent usually means an amount paid for the hire of a house, a plot of land, a television set, etc, ie a periodical payment for the use of something. To the economist, this is a purely commercial notion, which bears little relation to his conception of rent.

Ricardo said it was 'that portion of the produce of the earth which is paid to the landlord for the use of the original and indestructible powers of the soil'. Later, Marshall refined this to 'the income derived from the ownership of land and other free gifts of nature'. LAND is in constant supply and the amount of it cannot be increased if demand and, therefore price, increase. Thus, it is possible for a surplus to accrue to the owner of land because the supply is fixed and demand has increased. In this way the English classical economists laid special stress on rent as a surplus deriving from land and their theory of rent was evolved almost exclusively in terms of agriculture.

The limitation of economic rent to land is too narrow: other factors could also be fixed in supply, even if only for short periods of time, It is possible, therefore, for there to be an element in the reward for any factor of production which is due to a lack of ELASTICITY in its supply. This element is rent and it would not be present if supply were not fixed in some degree.

A temporary rent which arises from an increase in demand which cannot immediately be met by an increase in supply is called a *quasi-rent* (quasi = almost).

replacement costs. A term sometimes used in connection with the valuation of a firm's ASSETS. The replacement COSTS are the costs of replacing old capital goods (see CAPITAL) with new ones capable of performing the same functions.

resale price maintenance. The term used to describe the enforcement of a price by a manufacturer upon a retailer. A retail price may be set (i) by fixing a minimum below which the product may not be sold; (ii) by fixing a maximum which must not be exceeded; or (iii) by stipulating a price, which must not be cut or exceeded.

RPM is a controversial issue: supporters argue that fixed prices protect the small shop against competition from bigger ones with a TURNOVER large enough to make substantial reductions in their profit margins, and from those who cut amenities to a minimum and sell only those lines of goods in which there is a quick turnover. It can also be argued that there is a greater certainty for the shopper, who knows what the price of a good will be wherever he, or she, shops; also, that RPM can prevent a shop charging more than a stipulated price.

However, the arguments against are formidable. In the main, these are that RPM is bound to keep prices unnecessarily high and allows uneconomic and inefficient shops to survive. Such shops may, of course, have the virtues of being conveniently situated and of providing a personal service. But, if these are valued by consumers the shops will survive the abolition of RPM, even though the prices they charge are higher than are charged elsewhere. See RESTRICTIVE PRACTICES COURT.

reserve. A fund held for some special purpose or future occasion. A COMPANY, for example, will PLOUGH BACK to accumulate reserves, which become the amount by which ASSETS exceed paid-up CAPITAL and liabilities. Under-valuation of assets by a firm builds up a 'hidden reserve'.

reserve currency. The qualities of a reserve, or *key* currency have been expressed as 'the currency of a great trading nation, and one which may be earned easily by normal trade and whose balances carry the promise that they may be exchanged for goods both desirable in themselves and for the world demand which exists for them. Secondly, the currency must be stable in value, or at least, in a world whose currencies are losing value, it must lose value no faster than other currencies. Thirdly, it must be . . . supported in its home country by great and experienced banking institutions of skill and probity. And finally, such a currency must be free from recurrent scarcity. For this the balance of payments of its parent country must conform to certain structural principles, eg any tendency to run recurrent surpluses on current account should be offset by capital flows to foreign investment.' (Scammell).

resident account. A bank account held in sterling in Britain and owned by a person or firm normally resident in the SCHEDULED TERRITORIES. No restriction exists under the EXCHANGE CONTROL on the transfer of funds into such an account from another resident account, or from an external account (see NON-RESIDENT ACCOUNT). But, payment of funds out of a resident account into a non-resident one is subject to Treasury permission.

residual error. In the statistics of NATIONAL INCOME, the *residual error* is the item necessary to equate estimates of total income with those of total expenditure. It is presented in the figures as a form of saving.

Restrictive Practices Court. This court was set up as a result of the 1956 RESTRICTIVE TRADE PRACTICES ACT to deal with collective agreements referred to it by the REGISTRAR OF RESTRICTIVE TRADING AGREEMENTS.
These agreements are held to be contrary to the public interest unless proved otherwise to the satisfaction of the court. To do this, they must satisfy one or more of seven 'gateways'. The second gateway is the one most commonly sought; it is that 'the removal of the restriction would deny to the public as purchasers, consumers or users of any goods . . . specific and substantial benefits or advantages enjoyed or likely to be enjoyed by them as such'.
Most of the cases so far heard by the court have not passed the gateways and were annulled in consequence. In 1964, it was decided to extend the court's functions into the field of RESALE PRICE MAINTENANCE. (ie to decide if RPM was permissable in certain cases).

restrictive trade practices. These practices can take many forms, but essentially they all have some monopolistic element. A single-firm industry is unlikely (see MONOPOLY), but firms can combine (see INTEGRATION, MERGER, etc) to act in a monopolistic way. That is, they can agree to charge a certain price, or to restrict their outputs in order to keep prices up. They could also seek to prevent new firms from entering the industry. Distributive schemes are also possible, where there are 'approved dealers' who are granted trade DISCOUNTS; other dealers being excluded abitrarily.

Restrictive Trade Practices Act. This Act was passed in 1956 to try to deal with the problem of MONOPOLY and restrictive practices as a whole.

Part I of the Act established the office of the REGISTRAR OF RESTRICTIVE TRADING AGREEMENTS and the RESTRICTIVE PRACTICES COURT.

Part II dealt with RESALE PRICE MAINTENANCE, outlawing collective agreements, whereby manufacturers compelled retailers to observe certain prices, but enabling them to do it individually.

Part III of the Act removed the jurisdiction of the Monopolies Commission over restrictive practices, and reduced the number of commissioners from twenty-five to ten and its staff by about half.

retail. To sell to CONSUMERS, usually in small quanitites. A FIRM which does this is called a 'retailer'. See WHOLESALER.

retail price index. See INDEX NUMBER.

returns to scale. The LAW OF DIMINISHING (or non-proportional) RETURNS is concerned with the proportions in which FACTORS OF PRODUCTION are combined together and how the resulting OUTPUT is related to those combinations. Economists extend this to consider the effect upon output when the scale of production is increased (see LARGE-SCALE PRODUCTION), in the sense that *all* the factors are increased proportionately.

With such an increase in scale, the output may increase in the same ratio as the factors, in a smaller ratio, or in a larger one. These are called *constant, increasing* and *decreasing returns to scale* respectively.

revaluation. The restoration of a value lost by DEVALUATION.

revenue. This is virtually synonymous with INCOME, but is not often used to describe the funds received by individuals. The most common use is in public finance, ie the income received by government from rates, TAXATION, duties, etc.

revival. The period when an economy is recovering from a DEPRESSION (see also TRADE CYCLE).

rights issue. An OFFER of new shares that gives preferential terms to existing shareholders.
See ISSUE, etc.

risk capital. See VENTURE CAPITAL.

root-mean-square-deviation. See STANDARD DEVIATION.

roundabout production. *Capitalistic, indirect or roundabout production* is that which involves the use of capital equipment (see capital goods under CAPITAL) to produce more capital equipment. *Direct production* refers to the satisfaction of human wants without the intervention of capital.

running costs. See COSTS.

run on bank. An unexpected and sudden demand for the withdrawal of deposits from a bank. A 'run' is invariably set off by the fear that the bank is financially unsound.

salary. A name sometimes given to WAGES when paid to workers of a certain status (eg executive, professional, etc) at intervals longer than a week.

sample. A selection of data from a POPULATION.

sampling frame. A description of a POPULATION in the form of a list, map, etc, from which a SAMPLE may be drawn.

sanctions. Penalties imposed for the non-observance of a law, agreement or treaty. See ECONOMIC SANCTIONS.

saving. Saving is abstinence from CONSUMPTION, an exchange of present income against an equal amount of income in the future, or against the security accompanying a store of WEALTH. See also INVESTMENT, KEYNESIAN ECONOMICS, etc.

savings banks. These are banks which accept small deposits, on which low rates of interest are paid and which are withdrawable at relatively short notice. CHEQUE facilities are not normally given to depositors. See POST OFFICE SAVINGS BANK.

scale of preferences or wants. Because all ECONOMIC GOODS are scarce to some extent and the resources with which to obtain them are also scarce, choice has to be made between alternatives. It is assumed, therefore, that a scale of preference (or wants) exists on which goods have values relative to each other. See INDIFFERENCE CURVE, etc.

scarcity value. Where the DEMAND exceeds the SUPPLY of an ECONOMIC GOOD and the MARKET PRICE is high in consequence, the commodity or service is said to have *scarcity value*.

schedule. Usually a table listing quantities dependent on two variable influences. For example, DEMAND and SUPPLY schedules and LIQUIDITY PREFERENCE schedules, in which are listed the various amounts of money demanded at different interest rates.

Scheduled Territories. The *Scheduled Territories*, or *Sterling Area*, comprise a group of countries between which payments are freely made in sterling and for which London is the banker. The origins of the area lie in the financial dominance of London and sterling in the nineteenth century when sterling was in great demand for the purchase of goods from Britain. Sterling became an international currency, used sometimes for transactions which never touched its own country, with some countries making more use of it than others.

The Exchange Control Act of 1947 strictly defined the sterling area system, listing 'scheduled territories' in order that there should be no doubt whether a country was a member or not. Within the area, multilateral trade was preserved, but trade with countries insisting on payment in HARD CURRENCY was discriminated against. CONVERTIBILITY of sterling has, of course, removed the need for many controls; since 1958, residents of all countries outside the sterling area have been able to settle transactions between themselves in sterling and sterling held by non-residents of the area on an 'external account' (see NON-RESIDENT ACCOUNT) has been freely convertible into other currencies, including dollars.

All the Commonwealth countries (except Canada) are 'scheduled territories', along with Burma, Iceland, the Irish Republic, Jordan, Kuwait, Libya, the Republic of South Africa, South West Africa, the British protectorates in the Persian Gulf, and Western Samoa. These countries contain one-quarter of the world's population and account for the same proportion of world trade.

See also AUTHORISED DEALER, EXCHANGE EQUALISATION ACCOUNT, RESIDENT ACCOUNT, etc.

scrip. In general, 'scrip' refers to documents the bearer of which is to receive something. It is in this sense that a bonus, or CAPITALISATION ISSUE is sometimes called a 'scrip issue'.

scrip dividend. A DIVIDEND paid to the holder of SCRIP.

seasonal adjustment. Economic statistics which are subject to seasonal influences are sometimes presented with the seasonal influence removed. That is, the calculated effect of the seasons has been eliminated from the data so that it can be given *seasonally adjusted*.

securities. A security is a document entitling its rightful holder to money, goods or property. The commonest use of the term is for certificates issued to someone who has made some form of INVESTMENT, for which payments are made (see DIVIDEND and INTEREST). The term 'securities' is largely synonymous with 'stocks and shares', but, in fact, has a wider connotation, as the list below will indicate.

The CAPITAL of a COMPANY may be divided into 'shares' of an equal amount, so that the owners of them are part proprietors in a JOINT-STOCK enterprise. The owners may pay in full for these shares at the outset, in which case the 'paid-up' shares may be called 'stock', ie they would be the subscribed capital of the undertaking. Shares, on the other hand, are issued to be paid for in instalments (see CALL and PARTLY-PAID) so that an undertaking can receive a series of 'doses' of capital. This distinction has now become blurred and the two terms are now used interchangeably. In the case of the public debt (see NATIONAL DEBT), however, one does not hear the expression 'government shares'; it is invariably 'government stock' or GOVERNMENT SECURITIES.

The following are some of the main types of securities: BEARER SECURITY; BLUE CHIP; BOND; CONSOLS; *cumulative* are those, generally *preference*, entitling the holder to arrears of dividend or interest, before payment out of current PROFIT is made to securities not carrying this entitlement (see ACCUMULATIVE DIVIDEND); DEBENTURE; DEFERRED; EQUITY; GILT-EDGED; *non-cumulative* are those, again generally *preference*, where any arrears are lost and cannot be recovered from later profits; *ordinary*, which have no fixed rate of dividend but receive all of any residue of distributed profits remaining after the holders of debentures and preference capital have been paid (see EQUITY); *participating preference* are those which, in addition to the fixed preference payment, receive a share of the remaining profits; *preference* shareholders have a preferential right to dividend—see *cumulative*, *non-cumulative* and *participating*; REDEEMABLE; TREASURY BILL.

security capital. CAPITAL subject to the minimum amount of risk. See VENTURE CAPITAL.

security sterling. The residents of Denmark, Norway and Sweden may freely transfer sterling to their home countries, but all other non-residents are closely restricted in their movement of sterling capital funds. Such funds derived from transactions in SECURITIES or real property in Britain have to be credited to BLOCKED ACCOUNTS called 'security sterling'. These accounts may be used to buy, on a British STOCK EXCHANGE, securities payable in a SCHEDULED TERRITORIES currency and not REDEEMABLE within five years of the date of investment.

selective employment tax. This variety of *payroll tax* was introduced in Britain in 1966. The intention of the tax was a broadening of the base of the tax system and an extension of *indirect taxation* (see TAXATION) to cover the service industries and construction.

From September 1966, weekly payments have been made by employers who were divided into three categories:
  (*a*) those in manufacturing industries, who were to receive a refund of 'premiums' (through Ministry of Labour offices);
  (*b*) those who were to have the tax refunded, but not receive a premium; and
  (*c*) those who were to pay the tax and receive no refund.

self-liquidating. An INVESTMENT the original cost of which is paid for out of its earnings.

seller's market. A MARKET condition in which prices are high, ie favourable to sellers. Such a condition is usually a reflection of scarcity (see SCARCITY VALUE), ie when DEMAND exceeds SUPPLY, and buyers wish to acquire goods or services even if they have to pay a high price. See BUYERS' MARKET.

semi-interquartile range. A measure of DISPERSION obtained by dividing the INTERQUARTILE RANGE by two.

service. A non-material ECONOMIC GOOD produced by a person, firm or industry for the benefit of another. For example, teachers, musicians, artists and clergymen produce services. Services, as compared with material economic goods, are generally consumed as they are produced.

settlement. settling day. On the STOCK EXCHANGE this refers to the settlement of ACCOUNTS between JOBBERS and STOCK-BROKERS, jobbers and jobbers, and brokers and clients.

share capital. See CAPITAL.

share certificate. A document testifying to the ownership of a COMPANY's shares (see SECURITIES). See TRANSFER DEED.

shareholder. One who holds a SHARE CERTIFICATE, ie who has legal title to shares (see SECURITIES). Also called 'stockholder'.

share index. A number of BONDS, stocks or shares (see SECURITIES) are selected from a list of various trades or businesses and their market prices are added together to make up the base of the INDEX NUMBER.

shares. See SECURITIES.

short bonds. Short bonds, or 'shorts', are GILT-EDGED SECURITIES having less than five years to run to MATURITY. See MEDIUM-DATED and GOVERNMENT SECURITIES.

short-dated. SECURITIES with a life of less than five years. See LONG- and MEDIUM-DATED.

significance. A *significance test* is a method of evaluating the likelihood that the difference between numerical observations can be attributed to chance or not.

simple interest. INTEREST that is calculated upon the original sum, the PRINCIPAL, but not on any interest earned by it. See COMPOUND INTEREST.

sinking fund. A fund into which sums are put periodically in order that they and the accumulated interest will eventually pay off a debt or replace an ASSET.
See DEPRECIATION.

skewness. This is a lack of symmetry in a frequency DISTRIBUTION. When lower values outweigh higher ones a distribution is said to be positively skewed; and negatively when the reverse is true. When the distribution curve is symmetrical, the ARITHMETIC MEAN, MEDIAN and MODE coincide. See KURTOSIS and NORMAL CURVE.

sliding scales. A WAGES system in which the rate paid varies with changes in the cost of living, as determined by an INDEX NUMBER (eg, 'index of retail prices').

small-scale production. This usually refers to one-man businesses, or PARTNERSHIPS, or small COMPANIES. Such businesses cannot expect to obtain 'economies of scale' (see LARGE-SCALE PRODUCTION), but there are certain advantages. It is possible for greater regard to be given to detail, more personal interest and supervision, more knowledge of customers, and greater adaptability to changing conditions.

social accounting. This describes the MACRO-ECONOMICS—NATIONAL INCOME field. The economic activities of production, consumption, saving, investment, spending and earning are all performed by persons, households, firms, committees, institutions, charities, government bodies and so on. Each of these units keeps an account of its transactions in some form or other and these make up social, or national, accounts.

social capital. See CAPITAL.

social economics. This can be described as a branch of APPLIED ECONOMICS, which studies the social causes and consequences of economic behaviour.

socialism. A social system in which the means of production, ie CAPITAL goods, are owned collectively would be a socialist system; it would be socialism in an extreme form, and thus synonymous with COMMUNISM. Socialism is now largely regarded as a system in which a significant amount of the means of production is owned and run by the state. See CAPITALISM and MIXED ECONOMY

soft currency. This is the opposite to HARD CURRENCY, that is, it is a currency the supply of which exceeds the demand for it.

Special Areas. Under the Special Areas (Development and Improvement) Act of 1934, parts of Britain were designated 'special areas', but it was not until 1936, when funds were made available, that firms began to be attracted into the areas. The Special Areas Reconstruction Association was established with the power to make loans to undertakings in the areas and, by 1940, it had made loans amounting to £¾ million.

In addition, a special commission was given the power to provide for limited periods, all or part of the rent, rates and income tax of new or expanding undertakings in the areas and to arrange to build factories for letting.

See COMPREHENSIVE DEVELOPMENT AREAS, DEPRESSED AREAS and DEVELOPMENT AREAS.

special deposits. In 1958, the BANK OF ENGLAND outlined a 'special deposits' scheme, the purpose of which was to work in support of other monetary measures to restrict the liquidity of the banking system and thus the ability of the banks to extend credit. The Bank of England would call for special deposits to be made with them by the banks and these deposits would carry interest based on the current TREASURY BILL rate. They would not qualify for inclusion in the banks' liquid assets.

In 1960, the first deposits were made: 1 per cent from the London CLEARING BANKS and ½ per cent from the Scottish banks. This move was made to reinforce credit restrictions and in the following year the deposits were doubled. By September, deposits totalled £142 million. By the end of 1963, deposits were released, but were reinstituted in May 1965.

specialisation. This means a differentiation to adapt to changed conditions; an intensifying of the activity of economic forces in order that PRODUCTION should be increased, ie a more economic use of the FACTORS OF PRODUCTION.

The factor which usually receives most attention in this respect is labour (see DIVISION OF LABOUR), but there are many other kinds of specialisation: of processes; of geographical areas in extractive and manufacturing industries; in ancillary services such as banking, insurance and transport; and in ancillary trades making components for assembly industries.

See also COMPARATIVE ADVANTAGES, LARGE-SCALE PRODUCTION, LOCALISATION OF INDUSTRY and SPECIFICITY.

specialised capital. See CAPITAL.

specificity. The extent to which FACTORS OF PRODUCTION have alternative uses. Thus, a factor with only one use, such as a rotary printing press, is completely 'specific'. For most factors, however, there are varying degrees of specificity. Thus a nuclear physicist could do a range of work requiring less than his full ability. Generally, as SPECIALISATION increases, the greater is the specificity.

specified currencies. These are currencies which a resident in Britain is forbidden to hold without special authority.

speculation. The buying and selling of goods with the object of gaining from differences in prices. Buying at a low price to sell later at a higher price, and selling at a high price in anticipation of being able to buy at a lower price before delivery must be made (see BEAR), are the essential forms of speculation.

spot. For immediate settlement: a spot purchase of a commodity, currency, etc is an immediately effective one, as opposed to a transaction arranged for the future (see also FORWARD EXCHANGE).

stabilisation. Generally, this refers to the prevention of fluctuations in economic phenomena. For example, price stabilisation means keeping the price level steady; business stabilisation would mean the avoidance of the TRADE CYCLE; and wage stabilisation keeping wage rates from varying too much (see WAGE-DRIFT and WAGES POLICY).

stag. One who speculates on the STOCK EXCHANGE by subscribing to a NEW ISSUE with the hope of selling his allotment of SECURITIES at a profit as soon as dealings commence.

stamp duty. A tax, imposed by the State and collected through the purchase of stamps which are required to be affixed to certain documents. See TAXATION.

standard deviation. The most important measure of DISPERSION. It is the square root of the *variance* of a DISTRIBUTION, the variance being the ARITHMETIC MEAN of the squared differences (or deviations) of individual values from their mean. It is sometimes called the 'root-mean-square-deviation'. See NORMAL CURVE.

standard error. It is assumed that statistics (eg ARITHMETIC MEAN, STANDARD DEVIATION, etc) of SAMPLES taken from the same POPULATION are distributed in a NORMAL CURVE. The standard deviation of this curve is called the *standard error*.

standard of living. A concept denoting the amount of material well-being to which a social group is accustomed.

statistic. A numerical fact.

statistical regularity, law of. This states that a SAMPLE of data taken at random from a larger group, viz a POPULATION, tends to reproduce the characteristics of the larger group.

statistics. This increasingly important discipline has been defined as the 'measurement, enumeration or estimate of natural or social phenomena, systematically arranged so as to exhibit their inter-relation'. The technique used for assembling and analysing the data is called statistical method.

Also used as the plural of STATISTIC.

Sterling Area. See SCHEDULED TERRITORIES.

sterling balances. These are balances of sterling held in the BANK OF ENGLAND, or other British banks, by non-residents or overseas CENTRAL BANKS or monetary authorities. Such balances have always been held in London and include those belonging to other members of the sterling area (see SCHEDULED TERRITORIES).

See also CONVERTIBILITY, EXCHANGE CONTROL, NON-RESIDENT and RESIDENT ACCOUNTS, SECURITY STERLING, etc.

stochastic. The presence of a random VARIABLE or influence.

stock. See SECURITIES and GOVERNMENT SECURITIES.

stockbroker. A BROKER who is a member of a STOCK EXCHANGE, buying and selling SECURITIES on behalf of clients (or himself) for a commission. See also JOBBER.

stock exchange. A market in SECURITIES which facilitates the INVESTMENT of funds and the subsequent liquidation of such investments. CAPITAL would have less MOBILITY if stock exchanges did not exist; individuals or corporate bodies with funds to invest would be reluctant to do so if difficulty was likely to be experienced afterwards in converting the securities back into money. Stock exchanges mostly deal in 'second-hand securities', that is, the buying and selling is of securities already owned by someone else, who may, or may not, have been the original investor. Some NEW ISSUE work is done in British stock exchanges—see INTRODUCTION and PLACING.

stockpiling. The accumulation of materials regarded as being vital to national, or international, defence.

strikes. A strike is a concerted stoppage of work as a protest against wages, hours of work, conditions of work, unfair treatment of a worker, or some other dissatisfaction.

A strike, or 'walk-out' as it is sometimes called, is the most powerful weapon possessed by LABOUR in an industrial dispute and should always be regarded as a last resort, to be used only after unsuccessful ARBITRATION, CONCILIATION, COLLECTIVE BARGAINING, etc. See LOCK-OUT.

subscribed capital. See CAPITAL and SECURITIES.

subscription price. The price at which a NEW ISSUE may be purchased. This price often differs from both the NOMINAL VALUE of the securities and the MARKET PRICE subsequently established.

subsidiary company. A COMPANY subject to the control of another company usually because the latter holds a sufficient quantity of the former's voting SECURITIES. See HOLDING COMPANY.

subsidy. State assistance, in the form of money, for an industry. The purpose of a subsidy is to keep down the price of a commodity or service, that is, maintain a level of demand sufficient to prevent a decline in the activity of the industry.

SUPPORT for the agricultural industry dates back to the 1930s and subsidies are paid when farmers purchase fertilisers and lime, plough certain land, etc. Also, there are several types of grants for long-term improvements: improving buildings, fences, supplying electricity, etc; horticultural improvements; and land drainage and water supply schemes.

subsistence. That amount which is just sufficient to maintain a bare livelihood for a worker and his family.

substitution, law of. In a situation where the consumer is faced with a number of goods and services, his problem is to choose so as the *total utility* from the combination chosen is greater than the total utility of any other combination. Clearly this involves many substitution decisions; substitution of one good or service for another will take place at the point where their marginal utilities are equal. The *law of substitution* says that a consumer tends to adjust his purchases of different economic goods in such a way that the marginal satisfaction derived from them are equal.

For the producer the argument is similar, but he has to choose between the FACTORS OF PRODUCTION, judging by productivity rather than utility (see DIMINISHING PRODUCTIVITY). The law, in this case, is that the producer tends to employ the factors in such proportions that the *marginal revenue products* from each are equal.

See also MARGIN, etc.

succession duty. See DEATH DUTY.

sunk cost. See COSTS.

supplementary costs. See COSTS.

supply. The supply of an ECONOMIC GOOD is the amount of it that is offered for sale at a particular price and at a certain time. At different prices it is likely that producers will offer different amounts. At a higher price at a certain time there would be the prospect of a greater gain for the producers and they would seek to supply more—if possible (see ELASTICITY OF SUPPLY). On the other hand, at a lower price the gain would be less, and less might be offered in supply in order to reduce the risks involved (see 'risk-bearing' under ENTREPRENEUR). Therefore, at any one time, it is theoretically possible to draw up a table of prices and the supply that would be offered at each. This schedule could also be represented diagrammatically as a supply curve.

See also COMPOSITE and JOINT SUPPLY.

supply and demand, law of. This states that the PRICE of an economic good is determined by the interaction of SUPPLY and DEMAND. In practice, many factors can interfere in the MARKET so that the price arrived at is not purely the result of the relation between supply and demand. SUBSIDIES, SUPPORT and purchase tax (see TAXATION) frequently 'interfere' in this way, but it is still largely true that changes in supply or demand or both are likely to affect price.

If supply is greater than demand at any one time, the law states the surplus will generate a downward pressure upon price. And conversely, if demand is greater than supply, the scarcity will force prices up. It follows that there must be a price at which the amount offered equals the amount required. This is the NORMAL, or equilibrium, PRICE at which there is no tendency for either supply or demand to change. If a change in either or both takes place it will be due to some external influence—availability of FACTORS OF PRODUCTION, different techniques of production, production of a substitute, changed tastes, habits or fashions, etc—and a new equilibrium will be reached. The ELASTICITIES will affect how this equilibrium is achieved.

See also INFERIOR GOOD, MARKET PRICE, etc.

support. This is a general term for the assistance given to industry by government. In particular, it refers to the giving of a SUBSIDY and the guaranteeing of prices. A 'guaranteed price' or a 'price guarantee' is one that is made up to a previously agreed level by a government 'deficiency payment' on top of the MARKET PRICE obtained.

surety. A security, in the sense of being a legal safeguard against loss.

take-in. taker. In a CONTANGO situation, a person who has sold SECURITIES he has previously paid for and, instead of delivering them in the normal way and receiving payment, is willing to 'take-in' the securities and receive the contango rate for the 'giver'.

take-over. A *take-over bid* or *offer* is an offer made to SHARE-HOLDERS of a COMPANY to buy their SECURITIES at a named price with the object of securing control of their company. A take-over bid is also called an *offer to purchase*. See also AMAL-GAMATION, INTEGRATION and MERGER.

tap. A term used in the STOCK EXCHANGE for a SECURITY that is always available. It is sometimes applied to GOVERNMENT SECURITIES which will be sold by the government departments holding them when they reach a certain MARKET PRICE.

tap issue. An ISSUE of SECURITIES, eg TREASURY BILLS, at a specified price.

tariff. A schedule of charges for goods or services. But, more commonly, a system of DUTIES imposed on goods imported or exported either for revenue purposes or for PROTECTION or both. See AD VALOREM DUTY, GENERAL AGREEMENT ON TARIFFS AND TRADE, etc.

tariff war. The competitive use of TARIFFS by countries to change the pattern of international trade in an attempt to gain individual advantages. See GENERAL AGREEMENT ON TARIFFS AND TRADE.

taxation. A compulsory contribution to be made to the government. Taxation can take many forms, but it can be divided broadly into *direct* and *indirect* taxation. Direct taxation is imposed immediately on the person or body who is intended to pay it and such taxes are levied upon income and CAPITAL; for example, INCOME TAX, surtax, profits tax, DEATH DUTY, STAMP DUTY, etc. Indirect taxes are borne ultimately by consumers when they buy goods and services, but they are paid initially by importers, producers, wholesalers, etc. Purchase taxes and CUSTOMS DUTIES are the main examples.

We also divide taxes into *progressive* or *regressive*. A progressive tax is one where the rate of taxation increases as capacity to pay increases. Income tax, death duties and surtax are obvious examples. By and large, progressive taxes are direct taxes. Regressive taxation, on the other hand, works less fairly by taking from an income a greater proportion as that income diminishes. Indirect taxes are regressive in the sense that they bear no relation to the ability of the consumer to pay: eg an old-age pensioner pays the same duty on tobacco as a wealthy man.

A taxation system must strike a balance between direct and indirect, between individuals and corporations, and between progressive and regressive; must yield an adequate amount of revenue; have flexibility so that new taxes can be introduced; must not interfere with the country's ability to produce; must be adjusted as far as possible to the ability of the taxpayer to pay and must not cost too much to collect.

Taxation has become an instrument in the determination of economic policy (see BUDGET). But, beyond the main objectives of raising revenue and the redistribution of incomes (see TRANSFER INCOMES), taxes have long been used in Britain for specific purposes, such as the PROTECTION of INFANT INDUSTRIES or social purposes. Greatly increased government activity in social and economic fields has been made possible by taxation and a large proportion of the funds collected are channelled back to the citizens in a wide range of social service benefits (see WELFARE STATE).

The main forms of taxation are as follows:

CAPITAL GAINS TAX;

company or corporation profits tax—a tax on the income of a COMPANY, see *profits tax;*

CUSTOMS DUTY;

DEATH DUTY;

estate duty—see DEATH DUTY;

EXCISE DUTY;

INCOME TAX;

inheritance tax—see DEATH DUTY;

payroll tax—imposed on firms according to the number of people employed (to encourage the economical use of LABOUR) see SELECTIVE EMPLOYMENT TAX;

profits tax— a tax imposed on the profits made by companies. In 1965, the *budget* introduced a *corporation tax* to be levied at a rate of 40 per cent;

proportional tax—imposed at the same rate irrespective of the amount being taxed (rather like a compromise between regressive and progressive);

purchase tax—imposed on consumer goods in Britain in 1940 as a temporary measure to reduce consumption; now apparently indispensable as a revenue raiser;

sales tax—virtually synonymous with *purchase tax;*

SELECTIVE EMPLOYMENT TAX;

single tax,

STAMP DUTY;

surtax—a special rate of tax on incomes over a certain figure;

turnover tax—sometimes known as 'cascade' or 'cumulative' this is a possible replacement for a *profits tax*; it is imposed like a *sales tax* on the sale of a commodity every time it changes hands;

value-added tax—a form of *turnover tax* taking into account the value added by successive processes (see VALUE ADDED).

See 'BUILT-IN STABILISER', TAXABLE CAPACITY, TAX AVOIDANCE, etc.

taxable capacity. The extent to which an individual, corporate body or nation can be taxed without impeding in any way the power or will to produce.

tax avoidance. The use of legally permissable methods of avoiding the payment of tax, or refraining from taxable actions.

tax evasion. The use of illegal methods to avoid payment of a tax; also called 'tax dodging'.

tax exemption. A legally prescribed freedom from tax.

Tax Reserve Certificates. These are non-negotiable SECURITIES in which persons or corporations can invest funds set aside for the payment of tax, until the date when the tax is due for payment.

telegraphic transfer. A technique of sending money from one place to another by a telegraphed instruction from one bank to another, often in a different country.

terms of trade. A comparison of a country's imports and exports in terms of their prices. Thus, if the prices of imports rise relatively to the prices of exports then the terms of trade have become less favourable; and vice versa. Put another way: the terms of trade are 'moving against' a country if it finds that it has to sell a greater volume of exports in order to obtain a constant level of imports.
In Britain, the *terms of trade* are measured by an INDEX NUMBER computed from the import and export price indices:

$$\frac{\text{Index of Export Prices}}{\text{Index of Import Prices}} \times 100$$

so that a fall in the index would indicate an adverse movement. See BALANCE OF PAYMENTS, BALANCE OF TRADE, etc.

theoretical distribution. A DISTRIBUTION, the mathematical characteristics of which are known, that can be applied in statistical analysis. See BINOMIAL and POISSON DISTRIBUTIONS, etc.

ticket. A memorandum used in the STOCK EXCHANGE to inform the sellers of SECURITIES the names of buyers for the purpose of SETTLEMENT.

till money. The relatively small amount of CASH a bank keeps on the premises in order to pay out MONEY as it is demanded. See also CASH RATIO.

time series. A sequence of observations of a measurable VARIABLE taken at regular intervals of time.

token coins. Coins which have a metallic value lower than their face value.

token money. Usually, a combination of PAPER MONEY and TOKEN COINS.

total utility. See UTILITY.

trade association. A voluntary association of private business establishments entered into to have collective representation of views: to exert mutual control over trading practices; and to provide common services, such as research, market information, etc.

trade bills. See COMMERCIAL BILLS.

trade boards. See WAGES COUNCILS.

trade credit. A means of borrowing and lending between businesses. See *trade bill* under COMMERCIAL BILLS.

trade cycle. The trade, or business, cycle is a general fluctuation in the economic activity of a society, where the means of production are mainly privately owned. The fluctuation is from a period of prosperity, or BOOM, down, through a RECESSION, to DEPRESSION, or slump, then a recovery to prosperity through a period known as REVIVAL. These fluctuations are characterised by expansions and contractions in most aspects of economic life, viz employment and unemployment, industrial production, earning and spending of wages and other incomes, the buying and selling of securities, domestic and foreign trade, and prices.

In the last thirty years there has been greater understanding of the factors involved and of the measures needed (see KEYNESIAN ECONOMICS). An essential element of this is government intervention: history shows that private enterprise by itself is very unlikely to negate business oscillations.

There have been numerous theories of the trade cycle. These can be grouped as follows:

(i) *over-production* theories, which stress the periodical creation of surpluses and resultant falls in prices characteristic of recession;

(ii) *under-consumption* theories, on the other hand, stress the failure of consumers to absorb the goods and services produced;

(iii) *monetary theories* which offer explanations in terms of the quantity of money, rates of interest and levels of investment (see CREDIT THEORY, OVER-SAVING THEORY and UNDER CONSUMPTION);

(iv) *business confidence* or *psychological* theories, which underline the feelings of entrepreneurs at different stages of the cycle, ie their optimism and pessimism; and

(v) the Keynesian theories (see KEYNESIAN ECONOMICS, and ACCELERATOR).

trade discount. See DISCOUNT.

trade gap. See UNFAVOURABLE TRADE BALANCE.

trade joint council. As explained under DEPARTMENTAL JOINT COUNCIL, in 1919 and 1920 the British government took steps to apply the principles of the Whitley Report. See WHITLEY COMMITTEE.

The TJCs are concerned with questions normally dealt with

on a trade basis, ie in broad terms, wages and other conditions of service.

Trades Union Congress. This was established at a conference of TRADE UNION organisations held in Manchester in 1868, since which time it has been the national centre of the movement.

The objects of the TUC are to further the interests of its members and improve the economic and social conditions of workers.

It provides educational services: summer and week-end schools in production and management subjects, industrial relations, collective bargaining, social insurance and industrial welfare, and it is recognised by the government as an important channel of consultation.

trade union. The Webbs defined a trade union as 'a continuous association of wage-earners for the purpose of maintaining and improving the conditions of their working lives'.

In Britain, in nearly all industries and occupations, workers are organised into trade unions and there has been an increasing tendency for clerical, supervisory, technical, administrative and professional workers to belong to unions. There are now well over 600 unions, with about two-thirds of the members in the 17 largest unions (half the membership is in the six largest unions).

The functions of trade unions are, briefly, COLLECTIVE BARGAINING, mutual insurance and aid and political action (in Britain the trade union movement has many members in the Labour Party and in Parliament).

Trade unions are normally classified into *craft, industrial* and *general.* A CRAFT UNION, or *horizontal union,* consists of workers performing similar operations; an INDUSTRIAL UNION, or vertical union, has members from one industry only; and a *general union* is one without regard to skill or industrial attachment (eg the Transport and General Workers' Union).

See also CLOSED SHOP, LOCK-OUT, etc.

trading estates. An area designated for the introduction of new, usually light, industries. See DEPRESSED, DEVELOPMENT and SPECIAL AREAS.

trading stamps. A trading stamp is a document given by the retailer to the consumer at the time a purchase is made, representing the value of the purchase. Subsequently, these stamps can be exchanged for goods or money.

transferable account. Under the EXCHANGE CONTROL Act of 1947, a system of *transferable accounts* was introduced. These were sterling accounts, held in Britain by non-SCHEDULED TERRITORIES, between which payments could be made without the prior approval of the control.

See also RESIDENT and NON-RESIDENT ACCOUNTS, STER-
LING BALANCES, etc.

transfer deed. The legal document which records the transfer of
ownership of SECURITIES.

transfer earnings. Payments made by the state in the form of
pensions, unemployment benefits, family allowances, national
assistance, interest on the NATIONAL DEBT, students' grants,
etc, in return for which there is no *productive* contribution to the
flow of goods and services. Collections are made from the incomes of others by TAXATION and then transferred, out of
government revenue, to the income recipient.

Treasury. In Britain, before the advent of the DEPARTMENT
OF ECONOMIC AFFAIRS, the Treasury was solely responsible for
the co-ordination of economic policy, the control of public
expenditure, and the efficient running of the civil service and
other parts of the public service. After the changes made in 1964,
the Treasury was still responsible for the estimates of government
expenditure, the government accounts, the BUDGET taxation,
monetary policy and international monetary problems.
See NATIONAL ECONOMIC DEVELOPMENT COUNCIL.

Treasury Bill. This is a document by which the British government borrows money for a short period of time.
Treasury Bills are now the principal constituent of the
FLOATING DEBT. Before 1877, the floating debt was composed of
loans from the BANK OF ENGLAND and Exchequer Bills, the
latter being rather clumsy monetary instruments and by then out
of favour. In the mid-1870s, the government needed funds and,
on the advice of Bagehot, the new form of bill was introduced.
Treasury Bills are issued in denominations ranging from
£5,000 to £100,000 and are generally repayable ninety-one days
after issue; sometimes they are sixty-three days long. The bills are
issued in different ways: by tender, or by TAP. The tenders come
mainly from the DISCOUNT MARKET, overseas official holders of
sterling (tendering through the Bank of England), other overseas
holders, miscellaneous domestic tenders, and the non-clearing
banks. The subsequent allocation is decided, of course, by the
price offered, ie by the smallness of DISCOUNT the tenderers are
willing to accept. It is felt that government tendering for bills
would be regarded as unfair, so departmental requirements are
met each week by an allotment 'through the tap'.
Since 1951, the authorities have borrowed as much as possible
by medium and long-term securities to keep the short-term and
floating debt as small as possible. In 1961, for example, there was
a decline in the number of Treasury Bills offered, partly as a result
of government policy and partly due to the rise in the SPECIAL
DEPOSITS.

trend. A detectable long-term movement in a TIME SERIES.

trust. An arrangement whereby property is handed to or vested in a person or organisation to use or dispose of for the benefit of another person or organisation. In the business field, this has been adapted to mean an arrangement for the control of several firms to be under one direction. That is, a trade combination for the purpose of obtaining MONOPOLY powers.

See CARTEL, HOLDING COMPANY, INTEGRATION, etc.

A trust can also be a firm established for the buying of SECURITIES. See INVESTMENT and UNIT TRUSTS.

Trustee Savings Bank. The purpose of the Trustee Savings Bank movement is the improvement of the facilities for thrift and the increased recognition of wise spending and wise saving and of self-help and independence.

The banks are managed by bodies of local trustees, with managers who may be paid. The banks are inspected annually by the government. Their duties and responsibilities are laid down by special legislation and the rules of each bank must be certified. The banks can offer many facilities including: (i) the acceptance of deposits up to £5,000 and COMPOUND INTEREST of $2\frac{1}{2}$ per cent; (ii) withdrawal of these deposits, usually on demand; (iii) a Special Investment Department which takes deposits of up to £3,000 at a higher rate of interest for anyone with an 'ordinary deposit' [(i) above] of £50; and (iv) a Government Stock Department for the purchase and sale of GOVERNMENT SECURITIES.

turnover. The total amount of money changing hands in a business in a certain period of time, ie it is the total receipts in a day, week, month, etc. The turnover signifies the rate at which goods are being sold and is, therefore, measurable, in terms of the length of time that goods remain unsold.

uncalled capital. See CAPITAL.

under-capitalised. Not having enough CAPITAL; a likely cause of failure if a firm attempts operations without sufficient *money capital* and *reserves* or with an inadequate stock of *capital goods*. See OVER-CAPITALISED

under-consumption. An inadequate volume of *consumption* in an economy in relation to the volume of PRODUCTION. See KEYNESIAN ECONOMICS and TRADE CYCLE.

under-consumption theory of the trade cycle. If there is disproportionate expenditure on production (CAPITAL) goods (ie INVESTMENT) and on consumption (or consumer) goods, then, it is held, there is a lack of balance in the economy. If new resources or techniques are discovered, there will be heavy investment for a time, until demand is satisfied; then a DEPRESSION will occur in the capital goods industries, followed by unemploy-

ment and its associated under-consumption; which will affect other industries.
See also KEYNESIAN ECONOMICS and UNDER-EMPLOYMENT EQUILIBRIUM.

under-employment equilibrium. A situation in which total expenditure, that is, INVESTMENT and CONSUMPTION, in the gross NATIONAL PRODUCT balances with a NATIONAL INCOME insufficient in volume to employ all the labour in the economy.

under-investment theory of the trade cycle. See UNDER-CONSUMPTION THEORY.

under-production. A level of PRODUCTION insufficient to meet the demand for capital goods, ie INVESTMENT and consumer goods.

under-subscribed issue. An ISSUE for which applications to buy have fallen short of the SECURITIES available.

underwriter. An insurer; one who gives his name to an INSURANCE policy as guarantee of payments in the event of accident, loss, etc.
In a NEW ISSUE of SECURITIES, an underwriter guarantees that should an issue be UNDER-SUBSCRIBED he will take that part not applied for. See ISSUING HOUSE.

unearned income. Income in the form of RENT, INTEREST, DIVIDEND or any other form which is not the direct result of the recipient's personal effort, ie income from CAPITAL and other forms of property.
'Unearned', or *deferred*, income is more highly taxed in Britain than 'earned income', as the latter is entitled to 'earned income relief' amounting to an untaxed two-ninths of gross income (except where the income is subject to *surtax*). See TAXATION.

unemployment. The state of being available for use in PRODUCTION, but not actually being in use. Unemployment is most commonly used in connection with LABOUR and economists distinguish between several types:
  (i) *casual*—this arises where the demand for labour is irregular;
  (ii) *cyclical*—this is associated with the fluctuations of the TRADE CYCLE;
  (iii) *frictional*—because there is a certain lack of MOBILITY it is likely that jobs remain unfilled in one place at a time when there is unemployed labour at another;
  (iv) *seasonal*—caused by fluctuations in demand which occur regularly at certain times of the year;
  (v) *structural*—this is due to fundamental changes taking place

in the economy, such as the decline of some industries and the rise of others;

(vi) *unemployable*—those who are physically or mentally unable to work; and

(vii) *voluntary* unemployment—those who have 'private means' sufficient for them to do no work; those who find it possible to live on benefits from the WELFARE STATE and/or charitable organisations; and those other 'social parasites' who seek no such aid but still do not want work.

In Britain this century, there has been one particularly severe period of unemployment. By the end of 1932, as a result of the DEPRESSION nearly three million workers were unemployed, half a million of whom had been out of work for more than a year. Since the second world war, there has been a policy of FULL EMPLOYMENT and Britain has had a rate of unemployment among the lowest in the world—usually between 1 and 2 per cent.

See DEPRESSED AREAS, DEVELOPMENT AREAS, etc.

unfavourable trade balance. The BALANCE OF TRADE is *adverse*, *passive* or *unfavourable* when the value of a country's VISIBLE imports exceeds that of visible exports in a given period of time.

The difference between the above values is sometimes known as the *trade gap*.

unfunded debt. See FLOATING DEBT.

unit banking A system of banking where a bank's operations are confined in general to a single office, though some may be allowed by law to have branches in a strictly limited area. See BRANCH and CHAIN BANKING.

unit cost. See COSTS.

unit trust. Unit trusts were developed from INVESTMENT TRUSTS and were first introduced into Britain in 1931 from the USA, where they are called *open-end investment trusts* or *mutual funds*. The function of these institutions is that they enable small investors to spread their risks and obtain the benefit of skilled management.

The management company decides what securities shall be bought and sold and a PORTFOLIO is built up that mixes security with profitability. The company sells 'units' to the public, each of which represents a definite proportion of the trust's investment portfolio.

Unit trusts are of two types: FIXED or FLEXIBLE.

universe. See POPULATION.

unrequited exports. A term used to describe exports which do not earn any FOREIGN EXCHANGE; such exports can arise out of a debt owed by a country to another.

usury. The charging of an excessive rate of INTEREST on a loan, or any rate in excess of that legally permissible.

utility. In everyday speech, utility is synonymous with usefulness; to the economist, everything that is wanted is useful. The fact that someone is prepared to acquire and consume an ECONOMIC GOOD is sufficient and necessary proof of it having utility. Utility is the power, or ability, to satisfy a human want.

Utility is entirely subjective and is, therefore, not measurable. It is one individual's appraisal of an economic good in a certain situation. This appraisal may vary with identical units of the good as more and more of them are possessed, or at different times and in different situations. Thus, fur gloves would have different utility to a person in summer from that in winter. Furthermore, at any one time, a second pair is unlikely to have the same utility as the first pair. And a third might have even less. The utility of one unit of a good or service is called its *marginal utility* (see MARGIN) and the decreasing power of a good to satisfy is called *diminishing utility*. That is, as we acquire successive units of an economic good, their marginal utilities diminish; the additions made to *total utility* get smaller and smaller. See CONSUMER'S SURPLUS.

PRODUCTION and CONSUMPTION can be regarded as the creation and using up of utility respectively.

value. Adam Smith described *use value* as the power to satisfy human wants; goods having *use value* cost nothing to obtain and thus have no value in a monetary, or exchange, sense. *Exchange value* he regarded as the power to induce a person, or persons, to pay with other things of value for use of goods. His *use value* is a subjective appraisal of the worth of something, but his *exchange value*, or *value in exchange*, implies an objective valuation—either in monetary units or units of another commodity (ie a PRICE). Nowadays, we would recognise *use value* as being synonymous with UTILITY, but we would disagree that the goods with such value cost nothing to obtain. They would have an objective value in exchange, which may or may not coincide with the subjective valuation of the consumer, ie their utility. The confusion between utility and value has been resolved in modern theory by restricting the latter to *value in exchange*, at the same time carefully avoiding any suggestion of there being absolute and measurable values of economic goods.

value added. This is the contribution made by a firm, involved with others in the production of a good or service, to the value of that good or service. That is, the cost of materials, or the cost of the part-finished good as purchased from another firm, is deducted from the MARKET PRICE of the good when it leaves a given enterprise.

variability. See DISPERSION.

variable. This can be defined as a quantitative measurement to which a numerical value can be given, eg weight or income.

variable cost. See COSTS.

variable proportions, law of. The LAW OF DIMINISHING RE-TURNS deals with variations in the proportions of FACTORS OF PRODUCTION used by a FIRM. The law of variable proportions, or *proportionality*, is another expression of the principle. It implies that at any time, for any firm, there must be an ideal set of proportions, ie one which will yield OPTIMUM returns.

variance. See STANDARD DEVIATION.

variation. Synonymous with DISPERSION.

venture capital. *Venture*, or *risk*, *capital* is CAPITAL that is subject to considerable risk, eg money capital invested in a new enterprise. *Venture capital* is sometimes used to describe ordinary shares (see SECURITIES). See SECURITY CAPITAL.

vertical trade union. See TRADE UNION.

visibles: exports and imports. *Visible* items in a country's BALANCE OF PAYMENTS are those which are tangible, ie merchandise. See also BALANCE OF TRADE and INVISIBLES.

volume of credit. The total amount of BANK CREDIT that exists at a given time in a given economy. See BANK OF ENGLAND, BANK RATE, CASH RATIO, CREDIT BASE, OPEN MARKET OPERATIONS, SPECIAL DEPOSITS, etc.

wage drift. This is the gap between official wage rates and actual earnings.

In general, this occurs as a response to local rather than national conditions. When, in a locality, vacancies start to increase relative to unemployment a pressure is generated to begin or worsen wage drift. The existence of the 'drift' upsets established wage differentials and invariably puts pressure upon the nationally negotiated wage rates. That is, it is likely to be an inflationary influence.

See WAGE RESTRAINT and WAGES POLICY.

wage-fund theory. The theory that a fund exists for the payment of wages, so that if some workers get higher wages, others must get lower wages; if the number of workers increases then the wage-shares will decrease, and vice versa. This doctrine was used to show workers that it was futile to raise wages; some of their fellows would suffer.

Although it must be true that at any given time there is a total volume of wage payments, it does not follow that it is fixed in the sense stated by the theory. The theory stops short of analysing what lies behind the supply and demand of LABOUR; it does not distinguish between different kinds of CAPITAL—ie *fixed* and *circulating* and different kinds of goods—ie capital and consumer. Furthermore, the effect of the flow of funds through SAVINGS to INVESTMENT is not considered.

wage-price spiral. This is the name sometimes given to the alternation of successful wage demands and rises in the level of prices. See INFLATION.

wage-pull. See INFLATION.

wage restraint. This normally refers to the voluntary restraint from making claims for higher wages which might be exercised by TRADE UNIONS in times of national emergency or when an inflationary situation exists or is likely to exist. See WAGES POLICY.

wages. The reward paid to the factor LABOUR. The Ministry of Labour has defined the term as follows: 'the payment made to workers for placing their skill and energy at the disposal of an employer, the method of use of that skill and energy being at the employer's discretion and the amount of the payment being in accordance with terms stipulated in a contract of service'.

Wages are paid in two main ways: by time, and by piece (see INCENTIVE and PIECEWORK). Time rates are usually in the form of hourly, shift or weekly rates for a specified number of hours often with an additional *bonus* element. The bonus may, like piecework, be uniform, or 'differential', ie at varying rates. Again, like piecework, the differential method can be subdivided into 'progressive' or 'regressive', that is, increasing or decreasing as output increases.

As the ability and effort of individual workers can vary considerably, systems of remuneration have been widely adopted in industry that pay 'by results'.

The actual wages received by any group of labour may be arrived at in a great number of ways: degree of skill involved, amount of training, social usefulness, size of FRINGE BENEFITS, negotiating power of trade union or employer, governmental decision, SLIDING SCALES, degree of risk involved, custom and tradition, etc.

See MARGINAL PRODUCTIVITY THEORY OF WAGES and WAGE-FUND THEORY.

wages councils. In Britain, for a long time terms and conditions of employment have been mostly settled by COLLECTIVE BARGAINING followed by agreements reached without governmental intervention. But in certain trades or industries statutory regulation has been applied because negotiating machinery does not exist or is not, and cannot be made, adequate for reasonable standards of remuneration and working conditions to be achieved.

In 1909, the Trade Boards Act was passed to set up *trade boards* with the power to fix minimum wages in four specific unorganised trades. Later, more trades were added to the list.

In 1945, the Acts were repealed and superseded by the Wages Councils Acts. The 52 boards then in existence were renamed Wages Councils and given wider powers, including that of fixing guaranteed weekly remuneration and such holidays with pay as they considered appropriate. The 1945 Act and another passed in 1948 (dealing only with road haulage workers) were consolidated in the Wages Councils Act of 1959.

See ARBITRATION, CONCILIATION, INDUSTRIAL COURT, JOINT INDUSTRIAL COUNCILS, etc.

wages policy. A wages policy means a comprehensive plan or system whereby wages are established and regulated; *incomes policy* has a wider connotation, denoting an attitude towards all kinds of income (interest, dividends, rent, etc). These are not very clear terms and, when implemented, are carried out in different ways. In the Netherlands, for instance, wages policy means centralised legal regulation of wages; in Australia it is a system of compulsory ARBITRATION; and in Sweden, it means the centralised negotiation of wage rates between employers' and trade union organisations.

The essentials of an effective policy include:

(i) the avoidance of over-full employment (see FULL EMPLOY-MENT);

(ii) a clear statement of the intent of the policy regarding the increase in incomes consistent with the expected increase in productivity and the circumstances in which exceptional increases are regarded as justifiable;

(iii) the adoption of measures relating to 'non-labour' incomes;

(iv) the creation of favourable public opinion; and

(v) governmental action of a sort that will leave the public in no doubt that it is determined to implement the policy.

See WAGE DRIFT.

wasting asset. See ASSET.

watering stock. The act of making an ISSUE of SECURITIES in excess of the company's real worth, ie to an extent unwarranted by the company's ASSETS.

waybill. A receipt which shows the goods being shipped.

ways and means advances. These are part of the FLOATING DEBT: they represent day-to-day interest-free lending to the EXCHEQUER by the BANK OF ENGLAND from surplus balances on internal accounts of government departments and of extra-budgetary funds, such as the National Insurance Funds and the Issue Department of the Bank of England.

Government borrowing on *ways and means advances* is subject to statutory restriction.

wealth. Wealth, like VALUE, can have several different meanings. In everyday speech, it usually means an abundance of material possessions and this is similar to the economist's interpretation. He may define it as 'anything that can satisfy a want', but he is far more likely to refer to an aggregate of useful, scarce and exchangeable economic goods. That is, a stock of goods possessing UTILITY and transferability and limited in quantity.

Wealth can be classified in various ways; for example, into *individual*, *national* and *communal*. *Individual wealth* is the wealth of a particular person, including any claims or titles (eg debts and SECURITIES) he might have. *National Wealth* is the wealth of a whole society, out of which we could separate the wealth held by public bodies on behalf of the community (eg parks, libraries, nationalised industries, etc) which may be called *communal wealth*.

welfare. The economic well-being of the individual and the community.

The economic welfare of the community as a whole is sometimes called its *social welfare*, to be distinguished from *general* and *private welfare*. If a company is set up in an area of unemployment, the welfare of the firm's managers, the company's shareholders and the workers will be measured by the rewards received for their contributions to output; and the net output (ie VALUE ADDED) of the firm will increase the *economic welfare* of the whole economy. But the *general welfare* of the workers and the consumers of its product may be increased by much more than the increase in their economic welfare, as measured by the value of wages and net output. The newly employed may value their jobs more than the wages they receive; similarly the consumer may find that UTILITY is greater than price. Furthermore, the *social welfare* will probably be increased by more than the increase in the *private welfare* of those who receive an income from the employment generated by the firm. Transport facilities may be improved, associated firms established giving rise to more employment, purchasing power and so on. On the other hand, the new firm may emit noise or noxious fumes to affect health and cleaning expenses. Thus an increase in private welfare does not necessarily mean an increase in social welfare.

However, in general, economists accept that if economic welfare increases, welfare in general will increase, and vice versa.

welfare economics. Welfare economics is concerned with the social consequences of economic behaviour which are capable of being measured objectively and handled in economic theory. The technique of welfare economics is to work out the effects of certain causes on the size and distribution of the national income. Welfare economics concentrates on aspects of the economy such as the presence of very rich and very poor, MONOPOLY, and the lack of MOBILITY of resources. It is concerned, therefore, with an evaluation of how far an economy is achieving maximum welfare and how its performance, in this respect, might be improved.

welfare state. A welfare state is established when government activity goes beyond the provision of the essential services of external defence, relief of dire poverty, law, order and justice, to the provision of social services in order to increase the economic and social welfare of the community. In general terms: to provide *social security*. This involves the establishment of public social services such as *national* or *public assistance* schemes, *social insurance*, family allowances and other services providing pensions and grants; health, education and other public services providing benefits in the form of goods or services; and a SUBSIDY on housing, food, school meals and milk, and welfare foods.

Whitley Committee on Relations between Employers and Employed. This Committee was set up in 1916 with the following terms of reference:
    (i) to make and consider suggestions for securing a permanent improvement in the relations between employers and workmen; and
    (ii) to recommend means for securing that industrial conditions affecting the relations between employers and workmen shall be systematically reviewed by those concerned, with a view to improving conditions in the future.

The committee's recommendations were far-reaching and were to play a very important role in the formation and extension of British joint negotiating machinery. They extended the Trade Board (see WAGES COUNCILS) system and developed legal machinery for the settlement or prevention of industrial disputes. The recommendations were:
    (i) that JOINT INDUSTRIAL COUNCILS should be set up in well-organised industries;
    (ii) that works committees representative of management and the workers should be appointed in individual establishments;
    (iii) that the method of statutory regulation of wages in badly organised trades should be extended;
    (iv) that a permanent court of arbitration should be set up (see INDUSTRIAL COURT); and

(v) that the Ministry of Labour should be authorised to hold enquiries regarding disputes.

wholesaler. As consumer goods flow regularly out of producing units and tend to be bought irregularly from RETAILERS, a 'buffer' function has to be performed between production and consumption. This is the basic function of the wholesaler. He may be in business on his account, or he may be part of a big concern which manufactures, holds stocks and retails the goods.

working capital. See CAPITAL.

working population. This is that part of a nation's total population which is older than the school-leaving age and younger than the normal age of retirement. It includes those who are unemployed between these ages.

World Bank. See INTERNATIONAL BANK FOR RECONSTRUCTION AND DEVELOPMENT.

yield. The yield, or *dividend price ratio*, of a SECURITY is what it actually earns, taking into account the NORMAL VALUE, MARKET VALUATION, and the DIVIDEND or INTEREST paid.

zollverein. The German term for CUSTOMS UNION.